Five Hundred Years of America, 1492–1992

Rose Basile Green

Cornwall Books
New York • London • Toronto

Cornwall Books
440 Forsgate Drive
Cranbury, NJ 08512

Cornwall Books
25 Sicilian Avenue
London WC1A 2QH, England

Cornwall Books
P.O. Box 39, Clarkson Pstl. Stn.
Mississauga, Ontario,
L5J 3X9 Canada

The paper used in this publication meets the requirements
of the American National Standard for Permanence of Paper
for Printed Library Materials Z39.48-1984.

Library of Congress Cataloging-in-Publication Data

Green, Rose Basile, 1914–
    Five hundred years of America, 1492–1992 / Rose Basile Green.
        p.   cm.
    ISBN 0-8453-4842-6 (alk. paper)
    1. United States—History—Poetry.   2. Historical poetry,
American.   3. America—Poetry.   I. Title.
PS3557.R3754F58   1992
811'.54—dc20   91-58774
                                                                          CIP

PRINTED IN THE UNITED STATES OF AMERICA

Dedication

America who gives each person pride,
Above all shrines and ever rising steeple,
For all who have gathered from every side
You are the peak of unity of people.
From a heaven for centuries unknown
Before Columbus circled it to view,
Thy winds of liberty and faith have blown
Since accident of fourteen ninety-two;
To thee without a storm we dedicate
The gentle sounds controlled by beat and rhyme;
As Muse for each person would predicate,
May classics keep thy shape for all of time.

To live your history, dear U.S.A.,
Accept this poetry just as one way.

Contents

Sixteenth Century

Seventeenth Century

Twentieth Century

Acknowledgments

The theme and structure of this volume of poems are the resulting component of the guiding instruction of the late Robert E. Spiller, the incomparably sapient authority of American Literature at the University of Pennsylvania, who profiled my studies to earn the Doctor of Philosophy in American Civilization. Likewise, I owe specific gratitude to the directive guidance of the late Roy Franklin Nichols, also of the University of Pennsylvania, who encouraged my studies of the various supreme masters of American history who are too numerable for listing.

While historians must adhere to the compilation of all available actual facts and details, I have employed the poetic license of reducing the objective reality of the subjects of volumes to hopefully creative fourteen-line sonnets. Hence, this creativity deletes the necessity of recognizing by name the tremendous number of historic sources.

The sonnets compiled for this volume aim to give classical beat and rhythm to the development of the discovery that coursed to make America the exemplary nation of the world.

Preface

Columbus broke the path to the New World
Across the sea in fourteen ninety-two;
Like Cabot for Henry with flag unfurled
His search of trade would all for freedom do.
As when the lion seeks to rule the den
With how to battle, labor, and to feed,
So Kings in Europe whipped the why and when
The people had to live Their law and creed.
Above all force rose that of quality
That chartered Christopher to Espango;
Who dared for freedom and equality
To be American so chose to go.

The U.S.A. where all seek the ideal
Has made the phantom dream alive and real.

Five Hundred Years
of America,
1492–1992

The Real Discovery

America of fourteen ninety-two
Since its discovery became world known;
As Christopher by West the East would view,
The vision of Columbus hence has grown.
Natives of the New World had drummed their way
From North to South as tribes of untimed nation
Others from tyranny fled here to stay
While unaware of global occupation.
Names of who came historians now mount,
Who fame of the Discoverer would burst;
But of who rounded world by facts that count
Christoforo Colombo was the first.

Five hundred years mark for eternity
Discovery that led to liberty.

Quincentenary Port

Columbia, beyond the count of years
You hold the timeless torch of liberty;
As you lighten the darkness of all fears,
So you brighten all people brave and free.
You welcomed who fled from autocracy,
The minds and souls who sought equality;
As pioneers pursued democracy,
You gave their freedom new totality.
As sixteenth century your course disposed,
The race for heaven at your port was won;
Amerigo and Christopher exposed
Latins, Anglos, and Natives to be one.

He who first sailed the seas in fourteen ninety-two
Has moored five centuries, America, for you.

Five Hundred Years

Five hundred years at apex of the world,
America, for you all people sing;
While globes of nations keep most flags unfurled,
The bells of freedom from your temples ring.
Discovery of East by West to be
Columbus proved in fourteen ninety-two;
From tyrants you took ships to become free
And for all races warred to make one crew.
For centuries you have made bright the beam
That shines on stream that flows each day to you;
Dear U.S.A., you make come real the dream
To live the good, the beautiful, the true.

With half of a millennium now done,
America the peace of world has won.

The World That Was

When the route overland to East was closed,
Bright minds looked for a road by South or West;
To cross unchartered seas that need proposed
Was but the hope of dreamer at the best.
As in both Africa and Asia fell
Into the hands of heathens all their wealth,
In fourteenth century merchants could tell
That Turks could rise by more than warring stealth.
In fourteen ninety-two people were sound
As hands loyal whose gold bought property;
But a dreamer who felt the globe is round
Would make the-world-that-was seek liberty.

As Christopher Columbus had the truth in mind,
He, Ocean Admiral, the world-to-be would find.

Chris Pigeon

The peacock faced the boundless unknown sea
To test his own belief that world is round;
Like one who out of barnyard seeks to be,
He for the proof to find by trip was bound.
The route to East for profit had been closed,
And captains shipped on no unchartered seas,
Until one "Admiral of the Ocean" posed
As plain Chris Pigeon faced the course with ease.
Don Cristobal Colon for Spain sought gold,
Though Genoa of youth his faith had sired;
The genius that the Spaniards hedged to hold
Apocalypse of Ezra had inspired.

The Christopher Columbus, known by name,
An unsuspected world exposed to fame.

United States of Discovery

Columbia, America by name,
The nation by discovery was born;
As the Old World fostered the New to fame,
The *nomi* of first sailors she has worn.
Vespucci titles both the North and South,
While Christopher for happy land we hail;
Both explorers voiced vowels via mouth
That sings for ancestors who dared to sail.
While those from East of globe still seek the West,
They follow route of who first came by chance;
In U.S.A. they have realized the best
Of what once ancient Rome rose to enhance.

The great discovery in land of liberty
Is the recovery of human unity.

Admiral of the Ocean

Having Apocalypse of Ezra read,
He sought the gold beyond the Western sea;
Known by neighbors as Chris Pigeon, instead
He the Don Cristobal Colon would be.
The voyage then across unchartered seas
Was like a flight to moon at present time;
But one, an eagle flying over fleas,
Sought route by globe beneath the skies sublime.
As Christopher Columbus he is known
Who "Admiral of the Ocean" has been named;
That winds by West had to the East so blown
For the discovery he has been famed.

When mystic monks faced death garbed in humility,
Columbus gave his breath to world reality.

Bending the Barrier—Vincente Pinzon

With voyage of Columbus as prelude,
Explorers set their sails in every bay;
What from Europe to Indies did intrude
All sought the barrier that bogged the way.
Vincente Pinzon, one who had survived
The failed attempt of fourteen ninety-two,
At broad expanse of water once arrived,
Where flowing to the West it seemed to do.
Islands and shoals tangled him to return
To forty years of talking on and on;
The truth evolving from the shared concern
Proved fifty miles of river Amazon.

The chain of islands that a barrier formed
Convinced all Spain that the land was deformed.

Bending the Barrier—Balboa

In year fifteen thirteen a rumor spread
That direct route to China had been found;
But knowledge of Balboa stood ahead
About volcanoes and of world as round.
While on scaffold ordered by King of Spain
He knew that Atlantic was beyond rocks;
With the reward of death for all his pain,
He rose above the failure on the docks.
For King he had possessed the glittering waves
That proved to have more than a river's flow;
Hence, as he joined the heroes in their graves
He helped to time the truth the globe would know.

Barrier of Balboa was the rope,
A hanging for the view of future hope.

Bending the Barrier—Vasco Da Gama

For Eastern route to Calicut meanwhile
Vasco da Gama found a route direct;
But "finding something" some would judge as guile,
For dangerous voyage they held in suspect.
Cadiz, Palos, and San Domingo led
To Cuba for a sight of land unknown;
But Vasco proved the straiter route instead,
Above even what Prince Henry had shown.
"Terra America" some interest lost
As problem of growing geography;
The what and how to do was question tossed
Beyond responses of photography.

Decision was for natives to despoil
And leave the rest to wolves upon the soil.

Let's Go!

The question of new land was what to do—
Despoil the natives to enrich the flow?
Iberians yelled one great cry to crew,
One chant of Spanish conquerors—Let's go!
By theft they added land to New Castille,
Peru and Chile after Mexico;
Pope Alexander VI urged them to feel
That Christian blood need not make nations grow.
Maps of those days an image have outlined
Of South America and Central coasts;
But beyond that the reader does not find
The lands within where thieves became the hosts.

That who developed new world we must know,
Only to facts of history let's go!

Posthumous Fame

Posthumous glory like a lightning hits
Where no one has foretold how it might strike;
Although Columbus birthed a globe from bits,
In life none knew him nor what he was like.
What to contemporaries he revealed
Now in the New World glorifies his name;
In District of Columbia is sealed
The law that gives a statue global fame.
Along Columbian highways travelers speed
To reach a house within Columbian Heights;
From planet Mars a visitor would heed
All that Don Cristobal pounded for sights.

It matters not how many banged before,
It was Columbus who opened the door.

Course Columbian

While holy war of Reformation burst
Papists and Protestants to break the world,
Voyage of one Colombo was the first
That flag of Middle Ages hence unfurled.
Discovery of a New World destroyed
The feudal system that had ruled supreme;
The faith that the discoverer employed
Would make no people power seem extreme.
As a gigantic boarding house then known,
America roofed surplus population;
Its view by Christopher Columbus shown
Outlined what would become the greatest nation.

Though the discovery would stir more revolution,
In time recovery would course by Constitution.

Stamping the New World

Which nation on the New World put its stamp?
The question pried on for two hundred years;
Spain did from Horn to Grande construct a ramp,
While England on the land housed pioneers.
As France on Quebec pushed language and law,
Others on natives did their history thrust;
By its colonization Europe saw
What soon would world dominion make a must.
Though Indian Empire like the Roman fell,
Colonialism lifted New World high;
Democracy and liberty now tell
How people all as one with freedom fly.

From trading post through fringe and all-out settlement,
America set up the global parliament.

Via North with John Cabot

Caboto, whom we now John Cabot call,
In fourteen ninety made Bristol his home;
The New World for England he titled all
East of the Rockies stoned as a new Rome.
From Dursey Head he sailed the ship Matthew
On May the twentieth of ninety-seven;
The banner of Saint George he raised to view
On twenty-fifth of June in New Found heaven.
The fifteen days of ocean from "new isle"
Added for John three weeks for exploration;
But after having floated for a while,
He and his ships were lost for the new nation.

Since he to dominion first added the New Land,
John Cabot must with heroes of the nation stand.

Spanish Source

When Hernando Cortes his conquest won,
All history reversed in government;
The Mexico of fifteen twenty-one
Turned Spanish trading post to settlement.
The march from Vera Cruz to great plateau—
Capture of Montezuma's capitol—
Defeat of Teotishuscan—show
Power of Spain that was actionable.
Spanish America wore a new face
In New Granada, Peru, and Mexico;
With semiservile Indians in their place,
It helped the Spain of Europe strong to grow.

The New World steeled and oiled the sixteenth-century Spain
As nuclear power now gives nations global gain.

October 12, 1492

A full month out of sight of any land,
The sailors sought Columbus to turn back;
But he soothed all the signs of contraband
With cheer that they with voyage were on track.
Men, "it is useless to complain," he voiced,
"To go to Indies—with God's help" we must;
Then from *Pinta* by moonlight they rejoiced
At sight of limestone cliff that teemed their trust.
Twelfth of October, fourteen ninety-two,
From two o'clock with moon lighting the shore
Columbus until dawn rounded the crew
To island that he named San Salvador.

To wondering nations "Christ Bearer" made clear
That New World for possession did appear.

Primal Colonization

New mining empires opened to show
The depth and width of wealth of the New World;
Hence to America all wished to go
Where once only their escapees they hurled.
The nation, South and Central fields of Spain,
With semiservile Indian labor grew;
All that the exploiters had planned to gain
In course of time would change the old to new.
Greater powers all moved to colonize
Over the subjects stunned by condemnation;
The Dutch, English, and French proved to be wise
With transition from colony to nation.

For all who would decide on worth to cross the sea
America kept wide its gates of liberty.

Sixteenth Century

Columbian Obit

Columbus for all people stays alive,
As he to North America brought fame;
After his *Trinidad* let him arrive,
The nation flashed without sparking his name.
Though royalty of Spain had him despised,
Claiming discoveries useless to be,
All honor him who since have realized
What he predicted for humanity.
His final words voiced with the Divine Will
That he for royalty found "Other World,"
Whereby the Spain, once reckoned poor, would still
Its flag on richest country keep unfurled.

What Chris declared without exaggeration
Heaven has shared in growth of greatest nation.

Sailing On and On

In fourteen ninety-four Columbus sailed
South Coast of Cuba to contact Japan;
That Hispaniola was "Indies" he railed,
And this windsock to East he urged to fan.
Brother Bartholomew he left in charge,
While he returned to sovereigns in Spain;
Recruiting people free from work at large,
Rulers gave him relief for realms to gain.
King Ferdinand and Isabella gave
Three vessels more for Christopher to sail;
They did not know who would beyond the wave
Another corner of New World unveil.

Though offer of Columbus once turned down,
England soon sought to sail on ships of crown.

Strait Searching Columbus

In fourteen ninety-eight royal command
Led Christopher to Isle, his Trinidad;
Where now is Venezuela he could stand
With Indians who but with pearls were clad.
Last trip, his fourth, twixt fifty-two and four
Columbus searched for Marco Polo's strait;
He touched each coast all winter to explore,
Then tried in Panama for trade to wait.
The local Red Men drove him from the post,
Back to Jamaica for a year to lie;
Returned to Spain when having done his most,
Neglected and despised, all let him die.

Of all discoverers only Columbus knew
That freedom for Old World was waiting in the New.

Sailing On

We all now Christopher Columbus hail
Who proved the globe in fourteen ninety-two;
To East for haven all by West may sail
With faith to seek the best of what to do.
When he would not return when stars were gone,
Chris moved ambition to experiment;
The land that he by fate first touched upon
Made best of human culture provident.
There is no parallel in history
To growth of nation of the greatest strength;
Since first discoverer cleared mystery
Democracy expands to global length.

As in America unite all human states,
All sail like Christopher to open unknown gates.

The Name America

Amerigo Vespucci, Florentine,
Had no discovery at his command;
Like a director making real the scene,
He for Columbus staged the trips' demand.
In Florence printed letters have revealed
Vespucci captained voyages before;
From first of fifteen seven, then concealed,
He moved with speed to sails that numbered four.
"These regions—*Mundus Novus,* a New World—
Our ancestors had no knowledge of them";
Such statements opened like new flags unfurled
The spread of a new continent to hem.

Martin Waldseemuller insisted on the name
For land Amerigo Vespucci firmed to fame.

Pacing the Period

Europe's discovery and colonization
Of Western route roused interest most slight,
Until Peter Martyr praised a new nation,
Who did *Decades of the New World* then write.
Vespucci's lines and the Columbus script
Had not attained the dignity of book;
Readers disdained the words as manuscript
That would for Western route be like a hook.
To write off the New World and then withdraw
Spain almost did but for one teasing thought;
Some other country who a future saw
Might still achieve what the Spanish had sought.

What paced the nation first in 1492
Would in next century expand what Spain would do.

American Spanish Century, The Trading Post

Which nations would on New World put their stamp?
The question rose as how would power reign.
The first that to the road would reach the ramp
For a colonial trading post was Spain.
In Hispaniola had Columbus tried
What Spanish for a century would do;
Cape Horn to Rio Grande they bound and tied
What all had staked since fourteen ninety-two.
From post and fringe to settlement they grew
Until conquest of Mexico was done;
Europe then changed from Old World to the New
With the success of fifteen twenty-one.

The Vera Cruz to Montezuma victory
Made Hernando Cortes great man of history.

Adelantados

Adelantados, crossing east to west,
Had special permits from the King of Spain;
Like planters spreading out new seeds to test,
In exploration they made harvest gain.
Panfilo de Narvaez, one of first,
Chose Florida as field for finding most;
Losing two ships by hurricane, the worst,
For future he retreated to the coast.
With fleet of boats built from the native wood
Wrecked on the coast of Texas, down he fell;
Black Esteban, two, and de Vaca stood
Six years with Indians for tales to tell.

Those who reached Cibolà in Mexico
Stirred more belief than had the buffalo..

First French Setting

Condemned De Monts gave up his trading post,
The Port Royal he built in sixteen seven;
Most French returned to France with him as host,
Since his freebooting had lost them their heaven.
Unknown to France, an English band had sailed
Who Jamestown in Virginia had found;
In sixteen eight Champlain for New France trailed
To St. Lawrence on Rock of Quebec ground.
It seemed to French at first that all was over,
That New France would by others conquered be;
But Canada with U.S. would recover
As both with brotherhood made history.

As strength of Washington does the whole world enhance,
In Province of Quebec its magic bloomed for France.

Founding Decades—The North

Post Verrazzano, fifteen twenty-four,
And Champlain in Quebec in sixteen eight,
Waters of Hudson were cloven once more
With Henry and his Half Moon at the gate.
Though Cabot and Cartier had not survived,
And ships from Europe there no longer sailed,
In sixteen twenty a whole band arrived,
A hundred Pilgrims who freedom had trailed.
On renamed New England they set a post
Where leaders of Britain would future sire;
The Colony of New Plymouth was host
Of the English American empire.

Though the nations of Europe for the New World all fought,
The English colonies by trade their victory wrought.

Founding Decades—The South

Britains with joint stock company full strong
Subscribed by all classes, chartered by King,
Captained by Newport over right and wrong,
Settled Jamestown like post with everything.
Weakened by Pick-axe, illness, and starvation,
And ruled from England by council appointed,
Virginia, governed as London plantation,
By strength of De La Ware was thus anointed.
The colonists then marched for Thomas Dale,
Who stirred their faith in God and the new nation;
But they a stake in country sought to bail
Landholding liberty in its creation.

The trading post once hacked from overseas
Became Virginia of the Byrds and Lees.

Virginia Rescued and Rescuing

John Rolfe, who princess Pocahantas wed,
Seeded tobacco near the Jamestown streets;
With *Magazine* he kept Virginia fed,
As colony to England shipped its treats.
With private property an institution,
Tenant plantations grew from yards of ten;
Their politics kept breathing constitution,
A government of laws for more than men.
Virginia Company in London saved
The colonists from Indians and starvation;
By Magna Carta protected and paved,
Crown colony would be pattern of nation.

Virginia for New England paced its settlement
To make the Plymouth Colony first and permanent.

Pursuing the Myth

To Mexico in fifteen thirty-seven
The Viceroy sent Fray Marcos to sail;
With Esteban the two sought a new heaven,
As fabled Seven Cities they would trail.
Francisco Vasquez Coronado proved
By exploration this a myth to be;
In fifteen-forty his lieutenant moved
To make the Grand Canyon discovery.
By Texas into Kansas Francis pushed
For truth of cities and a strait to know;
When he all rumors had by facts ambushed,
He with deep pain returned to Mexico.

Pursuing myths as did Coronado,
Spaniards continued so to come and go.

Recalling Spanish Stamp

The Spanish in New World had the head start
With Mexico on left; Manila, right;
Before England and France, Spain primed its part
By 1580, when it reached full height.
With *hidalgo* and *dignidad* as things
That civilized with their diversity,
Mexico City and Lima "of kings"
Extended school to university.
On palaces and churches Spaniards built
Magnificence survived all later tests;
Though the *Spanish Armada* hurt its hilt,
The stamp of Spain on Western world still rests.

America that spaced from South to North
By Spaniards was thus traced for going forth.

New France

Traders and fishermen from France were few,
Small merchants wind struck by the change of kings;
For the first century's New World review
The story of New France is of small things.
Since Cabot and Columbus doors had burst,
The lock of strait to Indies needed keys;
Admiring Italy, Francis the First
Preferred a navigator Genoese.
For expertise more than Magellan had,
Giovanni Verrazzano was the choice;
Silk merchants of Lyons to help were glad,
Since route to China would make them rejoice.

The ship that would the unknown seas enhance
By Verrazzano sailed for the New France.

Giovanni Verrazzano

First port of call after West Indies sight,
On Cape Fear River Verrazzano sailed;
In March of 1524 by light
The New York site via the coast he trailed.
John proved that Hudson River was no strait,
Then rounded Cape Cod on to New Foundland;
For measure of the maps he gave new weight
To North America as the New Land.
The isthmus of Cape Hatteras was more
Than "Indian Ocean" legend at its side;
Giovanni was the one who mapped the shore
With facts that eighteenth century would guide.

For proof that the New World rounded the global tracts
Giovanni Verrazzano sailed and mapped the facts.

Jacques Cartier (1533, '35, '41)

Directing France to the Laurentian region,
Jacques Cartier sailed the St. Lawrence thrice;
From the Hurons who ruled each tribal pigeon
Soared wings with sounds flapping of gold and spice.
Chief Donnaconna voiced so strong a spell
With tales of one-legged men who flew like bats,
The Frenchman led him to old France to tell
The King who for more wealth sought newer pats.
Francis the First, musing for Mexico,
Hoped to put King of Spain out on the run;
In forty-one, with Cartier on go,
He sought the gems that would the whole world stun.

Canadian Diamonds were but pyrites
That joked Jacques Cartier to bended knees.

Fort Caroline

Le Moyne by water color visualized
The French in Florida with Indian trade;
Laudonniere with Outima fraternized
Beyond the view the painted picture made.
Once having pitched the post, Fort Caroline,
The leader for more force returned to France;
While some Frenchmen to West Indies fed time,
Famined others with Natives took their chance.
Spaniards in '65 captured the Fort
And slaughtered the survivors, every one;
The coast though studded by missions, each sort,
For passing treasure galleons was soon won.

In colony of French tobacco magnified
Herb sucked through cane with smoke that hunger satisfied.

New France II

A milestone in the story of New France
Was settling of Quebec as trading post;
Champlain at St. Lawrence made the advance
That over Five Nations made him the host.
He helped neighbors the Iroquois to fight
And by canoe the Ottawa explored;
The Huron gave allegiance to his might
To lead in the fur trade they had deplored.
Sailor, soldier, scholar, and man of acts,
Samuel "The Good Captain" so proved to be;
God-fearing man who blossomed dreams to facts,
His versatility hewed liberty.

Leading New Testament on loose morals to prance,
Loyal to king and Church, Champlain was best for France.

Samuel de Champlain

In 1590 Henry of Navarre
Ended Wars of Religion at Ivry;
For colonies of Canada, then far,
He gave fur traders a monopoly.
One Samuel de Champlain the coast explored
"Norumbega," now as New England known;
To find a better site there he deplored,
Hence chose to shape what Port Royal had shown.
He raised a palisaded habitation
And treaty fixed with Micmac sagamore;
With harvests dramatized as new to nation
He staged Indian pow-wows to voice for more.

While Old World vagabonds were given a new chance,
Samuel de Champlain was the father of New France.

British Prelude—War-Weary Nation

In fifteenth century England was frail
Though second in New World discovery;
Because of Spain she was inept to sail,
And France deterred her from recovery.
The eagles, English kings, had broken nests,
Because they needed grain from fields of doves;
The Parliament helped not their passing tests
To scratch like citizens who wore no gloves.
Anglos who to America did reach
Moved on the long, the hard, and the back way;
For expansion they did more than to preach,
And from sheer weariness they sought to pray.

With eagle flopping over with sway of a lost lark,
On ship of battled rover Britain had to embark.

Elizabethan Preface

Elizabeth drove England in high gear,
Expanding wide in wealth, spirit, and mind;
With Raleigh, Gilbert, Sidney, and Shakespeare
She reached for mounts of every size and kind.
With poetry, music, and prose supreme
Her hopes sought to equate the maritime;
While seeking India versed global dream,
She timed Utopia with New World rhyme.
On course of expansion her people sailed
To settle villages unknown before;
While with her trials to colonize she failed,
She prefaced the nation of open door.

In Gloriana's day battles indexed the way
For British Commonwealth to script the U.S.A.

Sir Humphrey Gilbert

Chartered to discover the heathen lands
"To have, hold, occupy and to enjoy,"
For Queen Sir Humphrey Gilbert sparked commands
Of men of four nations in his employ.
To found a trading post in Maine he sailed,
That would English possessions thus assert;
But while others from ship, the *Squirrel,* he trailed,
He was not of the raging gales alert.
As he on board was swallowed by the sea,
Sir Thomas More's *Utopia* he held;
This of America blueprint would be,
The Gospel of the words the dreamers spelled.

Republic of Plato with that of More in hand
Helped Gilbert thus to sight heaven with the New Land.

Sir Walter Raleigh

Sir Walter Raleigh, brethren of Gilbert,
Favorite courtier of Virgin Queen,
For Carolina was put on alert
Of where Amados and Barlow had been.
Knighted by her who lent the land her name,
To seek Virginia he organized;
But as England brought Armada to shame,
Caribbean was all Raleigh realized.
As he approached the land with songs and call,
Carved word *Croatoan* on tree he found;
Since depressed sailors there refused to stall,
They left the settlers and for England bound.

Of this "Lost Colony" no one yet knows,
Though with the Indians their blood still flows.

Elizabethan Course

England in New World had no trading post,
While war with Spain kept waging on the sea;
To fight all despotism she did most
Without the call of arms for liberty.
Had she become a military nation
Like those from Alexander to Mao,
Democracy would have lost its creation,
And no Virginia nor New England know.
Efforts of Drake, Gilbert, and Raleigh rose
Beyond what dominance of Europe sparked;
With global light that from torchbearers grows
Flame of Elizabeth led the embarked.

For British Commonwealth and U.S.A.
The torching Gloriana blazed the way.

Seventeenth Century

English Colonial Pioneers

Jamestown, Plymouth, and Massachusetts Bay
For English started as their trading posts;
But more than trade for England found its way
To make her people first as New World hosts.
While poor and unemployed sailed overseas
For furs, timber, oil, currants, wine, and gold,
Britain in Indies sought to find more leas
Where it a Protestant refuge could hold.
Virginia charter first in sixteen six
Declared for colonists "all liberties";
With birth and life in England as their fix,
Like eagles they nested new properties.

Settled with English rule for law and liberty,
The colonists for freedom sought eternity.

Plymouth Plantation

Though others failed, John Smith explored the coast,
Until the Pilgrim Fathers stumbled in;
Poor Separatists, who loan sharks had to toast,
On the *Mayflower* sailed freedom to win.
Brewster, Bradford, Winslow, and Standish met
A "civil body politic" to form;
How under rule of law to live they set,
As to self-government they would conform.
They settled place that Smith had Plymouth named,
Where birds sang in the woods with pleasant sound;
Like Miles Standish they farmed, and fished, and gamed,
And thence Thanksgiving with the Indians found.

With corn for beaver pelts as trading post,
Plymouth with Bradford was New England host.

New Netherland

The yacht *Half Moon* in year sixteen nine sailed
For Henry Hudson on river so named;
He, Englishman in Dutch employ, prevailed
Over the Indians by liquor tamed.
Dutch West India Company then bought
Manhattan Isle for sixty guilders fee;
The Dutchmen from the Indians so wrought
Greatest real estate buy in history.
The Netherlands had few to emigrate,
And Far East lands of Portuguese preferred;
They did with English first associate
When how for use of wampum they conferred.

Though Anglos used no arms to "beat the Dutch,"
Their peace with Canada had lesser clutch.

Non-Spanish West Indies I

From sixteen seven on to twenty-seven
The English, Dutch, and French tapped the New World;
New France in Canada sought to find heaven,
While Dutch on the Hudson their flag unfurled.
The English in America spread most
From Chesapeake, Plymouth to Caribbee;
While for the Natives they became the host,
They serviced them with future liberty.
Where Spanish eagles once had flown with power
To crush the sparrows who would dare to fly,
One Lord Carlisle for New World braced the hour
With rights for every bird to span the sky.

For common law England planted the seeds
That U.S.A. gardened with freedom creeds.

The Puritans

Mayflower Pilgrims to New Plymouth brought
Puritanism in its purest form;
Religious move the sixteen thirties wrought
Was righteousness of highest Christian norm.
No stained-glass windows, images of saints,
Did meetinghouses outside beautify;
With cool interiors all bare of taints
They would the congregation deify.
As English royalty with glamour pranced
And liberties of the people suppressed,
To a new heaven Puritans advanced
Where liberty would lift all that depressed.

Who in England could not with pure faith trod
Sought in New World their own City of God.

Step to Democracy

Charter from London to Boston transferred
Helped structure "a city upon a hill";
Life of New Testament by all preferred
Made Puritans succeed by work and will.
New England with West Indies shipped for trade
That sponsored freedom and prosperity;
A government colonial was made
Chartered with pattern of state liberty.
As they by vote created two-house court,
Freemen elected officers each year;
Body of laws and Bill of Rights as fort
Made "General Fundamentals" fight all fear.

Body of Liberties that fought autocracy
Made the once-bended knees step to democracy.

Bay Colony

Between the Charles and Merrimack their coast
The Puritans their land patent received;
John Endicott in Salem became host
Of those who Massachusetts Bay conceived.
Leverett, Cotton, Dudley, and Bradstreet,
Easton, Pynchon, Winthrop, and Saltonstall
At Cambridge University did meet
That they to New England would give their all.
Like swallows flocking while eagles pursued
Until in their own nests they could hold sway,
When Bishop Laud had them in England screwed,
Puritans opened Massachusetts Bay.

Ideals to practice free with some impunity,
The Colony would be a real community.

Spreading Colonies

From Massachusetts colonies soon spread,
As to Connecticut their spirit moved;
Then Roger Williams marched farther ahead,
Where he religious liberty approved.
With Gorton and Anne Hutchinson, the three
Settled as four on Narragansett Bay;
Williams to Indians then proved to be
The Christian who gave them freedom to pray.
Key to the Indian Language that he wrote
Started with "Cowammauch," the "I love you";
This spirit spurred five colonies to vote
As freedom States of England known as New.

While Old World Civil War continued on to brew,
The New World made good more with beautiful and true.

New England Settlers

New England in Confederation proved
What "Roundheads" were pursuing overseas;
The Puritans with chartered power moved
Self-government as best for colonies.
Farmers, tradesmen, and artisans combined
In workmen and yeomen community;
By home lots and the meetinghouse refined,
Yankees progressed with opportunity.
Their mother country Settlers still recalled
With love of fishing, hunting, and of sports;
The liberty and culture they installed
Was that of England spread by faith to ports.

New Englanders shared one belief in strife—
The Bible as their single guide to life.

Puritan Education

New Englanders for learning led the nation
By making the three "R's" a basic need;
Each settlement with schools for education
Insisted that all children write and read.
Knowledge of Greek and Latin was required
To think world themes and for college prepare;
Students of Puritans, who more desired,
Of good book, art, and science were aware.
For liberal studies Harvard set the pace
Of instruction by Latin disputation;
Theology increased all faith to grace
Freedom to worship Source of all creation.

Oxford, Cambridge, and Dublin all had shown
To Puritans the need to teach their own.

Faith and Work

"Never waste precious time" was the belief
Of Puritans who stressed their faith and deeds;
As work for one another was relief,
To be American confirmed their creeds.
Puritanism was the cutting edge,
Hewing democracy and liberty;
With place and duty breaking down each hedge,
The fields of work and faith made people free.
What New Englanders rooted has spread far
To Africa, Turkey, and rising world;
Each group in endless space may be a star,
As hand and soul now keep their flag unfurled.

While for first government each person had a choice,
Puritan precedent gave reason to rejoice.

New Netherland (New York)

Fort Orange, Fort Nassau, New Amsterdam
Became centers of merchants and patroons;
With farmers, clerks, and shopkeepers to cram,
They as New Netherland counted the moons.
Ill-tempered Stuyvesant peglegged his rule,
Making high custom fees a trading cork;
But Charles the Second from the English pool
Fountained for him islands he named New York.
All New Jersey the king sliced as his own,
While Dutch, Swedish, and Finnish ploughed his land;
The province from its royalty has grown
To give democracy a broader stand.

What to the king had been a liability
Was provinced as New York, a State of liberty.

Maryland

In 1632 the oyster war
Divided Virginia and Maryland;
One Sir George Calvert, Lord of Baltimore,
Was the most noble courtier in command.
Converted Roman Catholic, he grooved
The land that he for Virgin Mary named;
His son Cecilius with success then proved
The head-right system he with people famed.
Ex-rebels, kidnapped ones, and convicts came,
Ruled by "Advice, Assent and Approbation";
For free America they built the frame
Of faith within the Act of Toleration.

To vote, to pray, and join the assembly
O, Maryland, you first made yeomen free.

Virginia (1624–1675)

Yeomen farmers and rich men here self-made
Accumulated wealth in the New Land;
Sons of barons and knights of royal grade,
Sandys, Percy, and Wair had the top hand.
The first like Matthews with tobacco rose,
While William Byrd ruled Indians and slaves;
But as a seed to open blossom blows,
Virginia rooted blacks from white men's graves.
Cleansing their wicked oaths with Common Prayer,
From supervision they in South stood free;
But while mixed government they judged as fair,
They fought any with "too much monarchy."

Virginia, first as field of opportunity,
Was discontent to yield to king's community.

The Carolinas

With royal blessing Lord Ashley sailed high
To Carolina for nobility;
The Fundamental Constitution tie
Gave lord proprietors a rising spree.
In sixteen-seventy Captain Joseph West
Established a Charles Town for those in need;
Then Huguenots for freedom as their quest
Built a society with open creed.
The North of state tobacco cropped to run
But could not grow by selling of the land;
The Crown then made two provinces from one,
And each its own statehood then took in hand.

Though the proprietors sold New World to the King,
The Carolinas would as states make their own thing.

Non-Spanish West Indies II

Balance twixt Spanish, English, French, and Dutch.
In West Indies to Charles (Britain) gave strength;
Cromwell, Winslow, Venables—Penn did much
To give British possession global length.
As Henry Morgan conquered Spanish Main,
Sacking the villages, cities, and towns,
So Britain did by force the New World gain
And planters of Barbados fed the crowns.
When Spain to England thus Jamaica lost
With Montserrat and Nuns and Barbados,
The colonists to role of owners crossed
And spirit of democracy so rose.

While Hispaniola and Cuba were sacked,
The minds of people were by freedom packed.

New World France

All west of North in sixteen seventy-one
Was for Louis XIV of France possessed;
With native tribes Daumont de Saint-Laisson
Claimed what with Frontenac later progressed.
British and French rivaled a century
With trading posts from east to the far west;
While France was better at discovery,
To make communities England was best.
With wars French kings their men and money drained,
While priests from Puritans built them a wall;
Thus Frenchmen were in the New World constrained
To be loyal to king or lose their all.

British colonials with those of France set stage
For greatest power war in U.S.A. to rage.

King Philip's War

In eighty-five to ninety-five decade,
Woeful with arbitrary government,
A chain of "Praying Indian Towns" was made,
But unconverted tribes were evident.
Wampanoag, Nipmuck, Narragansett,
Once friends of Pilgrim Fathers, started war;
King Philip (Metacom) and allies met
To have the rule of Englishmen no more.
When battle passed its height with Great Swamp Fight
King Philip at Mount Hope sought his release;
But company of Captain Church with might
Forced him to fall for his eternal peace.

New England won but at tremendous cost
With villages and power that were lost.

Nathaniel Bacon Rebellion

War in Virginia took another path
From Indians to English overtaxed;
Governor Berkeley showed natives no wrath,
But white people hatred stood unrelaxed.
Noble Nathaniel Bacon took command
And killed Persicles, the fur-trading chief;
Rebellion of white men gave him the hand
To fight "Red Coates" who gave them no relief.
Defeated Nat at Yorktown found his peace,
No royal condemnation of his name;
His timed defiance gave reforged release
To proud and free who sang his cause to fame.

Bacon's rebellion won for good of nation
His victory of reform legislation.

New England Dominion

On colony of Massachusetts Bay
The Lords of Charles would force the Acts of Trade;
Dominion of New England grew to stay
Past the viceroyalty King James had made.
From oligarchy Puritan moved power
To Tory party, then an embryo;
For closer ties with Britain at that hour
Plymouth with royalty was forced to go.
All north of Maryland viceroyalty
Timed the Dominion sixteen eighty-seven;
But Englanders found it New loyalty
To freedom flourishing in fort of heaven.

What Stuart kings had shown Dominion theirs to be
Became New England known, a model colony.

La Salle

Robert Cavalier de la Salle of France
On Lake St. Louis had a seigneury;
As friendly Natives helped him to advance,
He claimed Louisiana primary.
While seeking Mississippi without fears
On March eighteenth of sixteen eighty-seven
He was murdered by rebel mutineers,
Who left him on a bloody path to heaven.
A patriot who for the French had staked
An empire for King "by Grace of God,"
The skeleton of Bob La Salle was raked
Where Texan vultures had upon him trod.

With fear of French, King James made judgment hence
That English all be one for their defense.

Revolution (1688–1691)

New England to the crown paid quitrent rate,
But feared the French in fixed-up "Popish Plot";
The Revolution sixteen eighty-eight
For Rights the Declaration hence begot.
Dominion was dissolved by Cotton Mather
With William and Mary by feast proclaimed;
But New York councillors would not gather
Til Jacob Leisler was their leader named.
Count Frontenac with *la petite guerre* raids
Had Leisler and Milborne by death defamed;
All who for crown of royalty were braids
For warring ties were by the rebels blamed.

Pro and anti-Leislerians in constitution
Prepared rising Americans for Revolution.

Somewhat Settled Revolution

By seventeen hundred most settlers were strong,
Enforced by Acts of Trade and Navigation;
Cases of conflict were judged right or wrong
By Privy Council of the mother nation.
Some of colonial acts had been revoked,
Like freeing each religious institution;
Puritan freedom by no laws provoked
Removed all causes for a revolution.
With royal disallowance in control,
All commerce of the colonies increased;
But when mismanagement started to toll,
New bells of future war their sounds released.

As noble English laws were mangled and profaned,
The Board of Trade no more could keep settlers contained.

Growing Colonial Cause

Colonial enterprise by crown controlled
Moved on with Board of Trade and (the) Plantations;
As matters thus by justice were extolled,
Britain built colonies while warring nations.
But like young lions with a leader lined,
Each herded group jumped with its strength of claws;
As system of disunity declined,
Each flock began creating its own laws.
A viewing Board the House of Commons sought,
That power of assemblies be curtailed;
But as Queen Anne in war with Spain was caught,
The overhaul of the New World so failed.

As course of colonies sought to flow more,
It rivered into pools of Queen Anne's War.

Expansion

Colonials from Maine to Georgia spanned
To Blue Ridge Knights of Golden Horseshoe fields;
Virginia and the Carolinas fanned
The "Old West" to export its work-force yields.
Products of forests, farms, and fisheries,
Controlled by Acts of Trade and Navigation,
Surpassed the plugging of distilleries
To iron industry that forged the nation.
The thirteen colonies of people free
Equated gales of both England and Wales;
Beyond exporting cattle and peltry,
Forges and furnaces heated their sales.

Though England would colonials restrain,
Americans stretched forth with all to gain.

Eighteenth Century

Boston Tea Party

Like Africans and Mohawk Indians guised,
Bostonians into harbor cast the tea;
The British government would be reprised
For the distruction of their property.
Mother England had twice tried to appease
The naughty brat on which she would crack down;
Coercive Acts of Parliament would ease
What Bairs, Burgoyne, and Burke had cause to frown.
"The dye is now cast" wrote the angry king
To bored Lord North who cared but just a bit;
The Boston Tea Party staged everything—
The "colonies must triumph or submit."

With tea partied for either King or clown
Bostonites led John Bull to a showdown.

Coercive Action to Independence

As Revolution may turn dreams to facts
That must neither in heat nor anger pass,
King George and Parliament moved law to acts
Coercive or Intolerable to mass.
Boston Port Act to pay for tumbled tea—
Quartering Act that soldiers commandeered—
Government and Administration fee—
All questioned the state power that appeared.
Remonstrance, resistance, and war outright
Made dominant issue be one of power;
Should colonies be held by British might,
Or had their independence reached its hour?

For each American the choice would be
"Where there is liberty is my country."

Boston Port Act

As on the private pleasure of a King
Subsistence of a Whole City depends,
Boston Port Act became the storming ring
That makes resistance thunder at all ends.
The first of June in seventeen seventy-four,
A day of fasting and humiliation,
Led burgesses to Raleigh tavern door
To exchange views with others of the nation.
Spirit of independence nationwide
Assembled in Virginia for resolve;
Jefferson, Henry, Lee, and Mason tied
By prayer what royalty chose to dissolve.

Committees of the colonies would meet
As Continental Congress all to greet.

First Continental Congress

Twelve continental colonies evolved
Fifty-five members to one government;
For one concerted action they resolved
So power settlement be permanent.
With Declaration of Rights statement made,
The Congress spoke for English liberties;
With the Association that ruled trade
They voted to maintain frugalities.
As Earl of Chatham said to House of Lords,
Troops from America should have withdrawn;
A loyal pond needs filling of the fords
While it with liberty the brooks would spawn.

Had Continental Congress thus been recognized,
There would have been no war with Great Britain devised.

Chatham's Bill

The Earl of Chatham fired by oration
The wisdom and patience of U.S.A.;
He spoke for bill for reconciliation
And have Coercive Acts silenced away.
He would have parliamentary control,
But hold the Continental Congress seat;
Though he for settling troubles would enroll,
His principles met a rounded defeat.
Had Chatham's Bill been passed in seventy-five,
In which each point of practice was a star,
For Independence none would have to strive,
Nor would the colonies have marched to war.

As reconciliation no longer was a fact,
New England soon was bound by the Restraining Act.

New England Restraining Act

Restraining Act kept New England in bond,
Forbidding the four colonies to trade
On any brook not of maternal pond
Nor near a pool that other rivers made.
The Act to fishermen access forbade
On Nova Scotia, Newfoundland, to bank;
Yankees deprived of fisheries were frayed
Like dolphins forced to twist within a tank.
The "sacred codfish" were a cause of war,
As two nations moved in martial array;
While General Gage was rising like a star,
The winds of revolution dawned the day.

The colonies with peace could not relax
While Parliament pressed on with tax on tax.

First Act of American War

Like Daniel Boone, "long hunters" pushed to west,
Past hardwood forests, meadows, and blue grass,
While Shawnee in Virginia fought their best
Til Chief Cornstalk could not Point Pleasant pass.
Assembly at Concord in seventy-four
Had John Hancock chosen as president,
While Paul Revere and others rode for war
Pitcairn at Lexington made evident.
Farmers against British then took their stand
To fire the first "shot heard round the world";
From patriots the whole world felt the hand
That had the flag of freedom now unfurled.

Anticolonials fought first successful war
That voiced the "words that shall echo forevermore."

Second Congress Olive Branch

The Second Continental Congress met
In Philadelphia, May, seventy-five;
Hence, for *republic* colonies were set
For Bunker Hill spirit to keep alive.
Union by Olive Branch Petition sought
A lasting happy reconciliation;
King George ordered endeavors to be naught,
Suppressing traitors of rebelling nation.
Although John Bull did not to rebels yield,
America on *Alfred* flew its flag;
As Washington bore thirteen stripes in field,
His strength for Union Jack suffered no lag.

Since branch of peace Great Britain would not leaven,
The Stars and Stripes rose high in seventy-seven.

Declaration of Independence

Convinced by *Common Sense* of Thomas Paine,
The thirteen colonies their freedom sought;
Flaming of Falmouth and Norfolk helped gain
The strength to move from what Britain had wrought.
Adams, Franklin, Sherman, and Livingston
With Jefferson prepared the Declaration;
Second Treatise of Government thus done
Proved John Locke verbalizer of the nation.
United as America by name,
The States their lives to "Sacred Honor" pledged;
Their Declaration for the world became
The voice for freedom where all people hedged.

Rights unalienable from the Creator stress
Life, Liberty, and the Pursuit of Happiness.

1775

The war for independence struggled on
With Washington of brave tenacity;
Enlistment for three years past pro and con
Gave U.S. battling its capacity.
With Wayne, Morgan, Howard, plus Knox and Greene
George won three-year enlistment for his men;
The Thirteen Colonies by world were seen
As rising nation seeking place and when.
While strifes at Concord and at Bunker Hill
Stirred farmers of the nation with alarm,
Later with reason to partake of kill
They said, "We'll see who's goin' t' own this farm."

Fatiguemen, mariners, oarsmen, and pioneers,
The Continental Army unified as peers.

Financial and Foreign Aid

Soldiers who War of Independence fought
Were badly tended, clothed, and scarcely fed;
At darkest time one ray of light was wrought
By Robert Morris who finances led.
Who bank of North America first found
Made country on hard-money basis strong;
This foreign volunteer made nation sound
By leading troops to know the right from wrong.
De Lafayette, Kosciuszko, Duportail,
Pulaski, de Kalb, and von Steuben—all
Helped Continental Army to prevail
In test that Monmouth readied them for call.

As foreign volunteers drilled the U.S.A.,
The Continentals stilled Britains in every way.

Colonial Weapons

Muskets, shotguns, rifles mixed with carbines
Armed the first soldiers of the colonies;
On shipboard "leathernecks" protected lines
That brought the British army to its knees.
Light infantry of Washington scored high,
Wearing leather helmet and horsehair crest;
What Lafayette and Hamilton would try
Knox proved artillery to don the best.
The cannon that shot a "12-pounder" ball
Was aided by mortars exploding fire;
"Legions" of mounted units did their all
While troopers fought on feet above the mire.

"Light Horne Harry" Lee and the leader Pulaski
Proved how the foot with strength like any gun could be.

Sea Strength

On warships Britain had its greatest strength
With troops lined from England to U.S.A.;
From Hartford Town to Florida full length
Navies of separate States banked their own way.
When Congress founded its own fleet to sail
With Robert Morris and Cap John Paul Jones,
It was like Romans whom historians hail,
Who reduced Carthage to level of stones.
On state, private, and Continental ships
Captains sailed only to capture the prize;
When goods with war market then came to grips,
French royal navy gave the sea new size.

Sailors decided while they were at sea
Who Loyalists or Patriots would be.

American Patriots and Loyalists

By enemies they were as Tories known,
Americans who gave Britain support;
These Loyalists to colonies had shown
That they with mother country would consort.
Butler's Rangers and Johnson's Loyal Greens
Massacred Wyoming farmers of peace;
But Patriots would battle Kings and Queens
Who to freedom lovers gave no release.
Contending parties thus lived side by side
Throughout the length and width of the whole land;
Their civil war forced nation to divide
More than did independence as their stand.

American parties each wore on foot
As Patriots or Loyalists the boot.

Commander in Chief George Washington

Integrity of character and strength
In politics and military role
George Washington embodies to full length
With sacrifice of both body and soul.
Placating troops unpaid, hungry, and cold,
He led his soldiers with a warmth of style;
Beyond "Conway Cabal" he kept on hold
Affection and respect of rank and file.
Without the fancy lip of royalty,
For chief commander swords were girded on;
The military rose with loyalty
For action for the brave George Washington.

Armies of people conquer cause of grief
When who to war for justice is the chief.

New York Colonial Campaign

New York, like Penn's City, an empty port,
Might have by William Howe been won for King;
When Washington made Manhattan his fort,
The British had cordons on everything.
With Generals Israel Putnam and Charles Lee
Commander on the Hudson planned his course;
Before Cornwallis they all had to flee
From Palisades cannoned by Hessian force.
Though Battle of Long Island spelled defeat,
George Washington with strategy moved back;
Since he the army saved by this retreat,
He was able in future to attack.

Though from New York the rebel army fled,
On to New Jersey colonists were led.

Jersey Advance

Before Cornwallis George New Jersey crossed
Where Hessians had looted the homes and shops;
With rising sun on Christmas Day he tossed
The winds of victory past Trenton props.
From Princeton he went forth to Morristown,
Marching with raids that saved the nation's cause;
With Hackensack, Newark, Elizabethtown,
The conquest will forever stir applause.
The greatest gentleman of U.S.A.
Proved equally to be genius of war;
For all tested by time then and today
George Washington remains the guiding star.

As the campaign to Jersies made advance,
So Freedom will all patriots enhance.

Saratoga Turning Point

Strength at Battle of Bennington exposed
What North American Army could reach;
Vermont Green Mountain Boys Schyler opposed
To stop Burgoyne who hopped with jump and speech.
Battle of Freeman's Farm on Bemis Heights
Forced loyalist to float a flag of truce;
The eagle to the doves surrendered sites
That would the nests for freedom flocks produce.
All who surrendered scored the victory when,
With Gates as top commander and the star,
Three hundred officers, thousands of men,
For colonies made turning point of war.

From "Hampshire Grants" to both the left and right
Surrender of Burgoyne turned course of might.

Winner Washington

Defeat at Brandywine and Germantown
Made Washington return to Valley Forge;
Conway Cabol tried to prove him a clown,
But country and the army stood by George.
Surrender of Burgoyne the British urged
To put Henry Clinton in place of Howe;
Then Battle of Monmouth all service surged
To swell the Chief Commander at its prow.
As he New York encircled on each side,
Hoping that fleet of French would break stalemate,
George Washington remained the people's pride
While he for land of freedom held the gate.

The General whose patience was most evident
Became victor for nation and first president.

French Alliance

One of "other parts" of the world was France
Whose aid the Continental Congress sought;
As high ideals do warriors enhance,
So French intelligentsia was wrought.
As Franklin's *Way to Wealth* the French court won,
The sweet society with treaties veered;
Had Count d'Estaing by British not been done,
Cornwallis at Yorktown would have been cheered.
Assault in October for Admiral lost
The cause for which Pulaski had been killed;
Unanchoraged Frenchmen the ocean crossed
With purpose of alliance unfulfilled.

One year and half with no French at the gate,
The war for freedom reached a low stalemate.

Haphazard Raids

War at stalemate stirred raids fought bat-and-run
By scores of British ships at New York docked;
To terrify the Yankees all was done
To keep the "countryside in arms" full locked.
When Sir George Collier, having townships burned,
Would sail through Hell Gate to Long Island Sound,
The countryside for its defense all turned
To Captain John Paul Jones to save the ground.
With *Ranger* Jones had captained Britain's *Drake,*
Then with *Bonhomme Richard* had rounded strength;
Under the Stars and Stripes all saw him take
He sailed around the British Isles full length.

Haphazard though the raids had seemed to be,
They stirred the colonies to victory.

Campaign in Carolinas

In early seventeen-eighty Charleston fell,
Followed by Gates' defeat at Camden near;
Then, like the devil dickering for hell,
Benedict Arnold served Clinton a year.
Lord Cornwallis took battle to the South,
Where Ferguson on Kings Mountain was topped;
When Greene for Washington with more than mouth
Divided troops, his strategy was hopped.
From the Cowpens, Dan River, Guilford meet
All Britainists to Charleston did return;
From Lafayette defeat Lord sought retreat
To Malvern Hill for future flames to burn.

Mighty events both on the sea and land
From Carolinas gave nation its stand.

Yorktown

On dark of States shone a new torch from France
From King on Washington and Rochambeau;
De Grasse at Chesapeake would take the chance
And then to Yorktown carry the flambeau.
The siege followed the book of warring lines,
As chief commander with the French conferred;
With horn-works, mines, trenches, and countermines
Future advance of British they deferred.
Cornwallis knew when to withdraw his packs
As "World Turned Upside Down" without alarms;
Gallant sorties and strong counterattacks
Forced British regiments to lay down arms.

"The play is over" announced Lafayette
As from Yorktown the curtain pull was set.

Conclusion of Revolution

Tories and Indians last battle fought
At Bryan's Station, fort near Lexington;
Beating Shawnees to George Rogers Clark brought
The force of freedom led by Washington.
The end of war in seventeen eighty-two
Precluded Peace of Paris for the world;
With winds of Franklin stirring all the view,
The flag of independence was unfurled.
The new republic was by liberals hailed,
Who deemed it savior from royalty;
Control of its own fate that it entailed
Would free reason to rule equality.

Triumph of the Republic was the seed
That would the freedom of all nations breed.

Freedom Personified

Reason may give perception size and length
With words spoken or typed with current print;
But it must bring to view its shape and strength
In person that embodies every hint.
As Washington for land of freedom marched,
His troops looked weather-beaten and forlorn;
But royalty had not the General starched,
Nor would he have the robes of kingship worn.
After George left and rowed to Paulus Hook,
From home he gave Congress his resignation;
A living statue above every nook,
He was the flesh and blood of the new nation.

In all the real of dreams in world he won
Each person visions one George Washington.

Bill of Rights

Most revolutions with a despot end,
Who thrashes liberty to size of straw;
America was first from stalks to bend
A government with freedom stacked by law.
Leaders of colonies were learned men
Like Plato, Aristotle, Cicero;
Jefferson, Adams, Bowdoin, Madison
The boat of Constitution all could row.
"Unchangeable, unwritten laws of heaven"
From Sophocles to words of States gave light;
Equality and freedom hence to leaven
Coursed commonwealth to court the Bill of Rights.

The growing nation gained power by pen
For government of laws and not of men.

Frames of Government

Three frames structured first government of States:
Virginian legislative's supreme door—
Pennsylvanian unicameral gates—
"Mixed" Massachusetts types from every floor.
Conservative reaction from all rose
With "checks and balances" controlling strength;
As gardens blossom with the wind that blows,
Freedom by law flowered with proper length.
People with genius for self-government
Followed who politics a science made;
Docile and critical in fundament,
Frontiersmen drafted nation to their grade.

One Penn State's constitution "rational"
Framed institutions international.

Confederacy

True freedom balanced with authority
Is like the sun in harmony with rain;
To clear the air for the majority
Confederation must states rights retain.
Land grabbers, clouds before a rising storm,
Negotiations with Congress engaged;
When Maryland gave Articles their form,
First Constitution with sunshine was staged.
Great Seal of the United States was stamped
While eagles flew from once imperial Rome;
Novus Ordo seclorum thus was ramped
As now America became its home.

Confederacy on independence porch
For *nova progenies* carried the torch.

Independence Day

E Pluribus Unum the nation rose,
An eagle crowned by light of thirteen stars;
As constellation of free people grows,
The symbol strengthens peace once paced by Mars.
On July fourth in seventeen seventy-six
In Penn's City in Independence Hall
The Declaration Articles did fix
Great Seal of U.S.A. to view of all.
As Divine Providence favored its norm
With olive branch and arrows as its keys,
The eagle gave to freedom size and form
To fly "A New Cycle of Centuries."

As global unity for equal rights flies high,
Let all the people pray for the fourth of July.

Colonial Commercial Revival

With peace and independence as their fort,
The colonies lost their imperial trade;
They sold to Orientals at their port
The iron tools and knickknacks that they made.
Postwar revival rode a special horse
Like "Royal Gift" from Spain to Washington;
Classics of turf in England followed course
For mare America to breed a son.
One stallion, Justice Morgan, was of best,
A model that became the people's choice;
For race and work he passed each growing test
That made farmers, soldiers, and all rejoice.

As trail of track with classic sod survived,
The race for commerce in new land revived.

Postwar Settlement

Brave Loyalists to U.S.A. returned
To be commanders of communities;
As prewar debts to Britain most States spurned,
The land invited opportunities.
Infant republic was pressured by Spain,
Who checked America both south and west;
With Indian raiding settlements to gain,
The backwoods went to Spanish in the test.
America by revolution freed
Might still by statesmanship have been confined;
A narrow strip might have chartered its creed
Twixt Canada and Florida outlined.

Postwar leaders showed by their ruling hand
How Independence would maintain the land.

American Culture Dayspring

Young colonists pursued knowledge and arts
With words of Webster weaving books and sound;
Joel Barlow and Phil Freneau were starts
Ex-slave Phillis Wheatley brought to full round.
Trumbull and Peale portrayed the time with paint,
While Rittenhouse professed astronomy;
Knowledge in print produced more than one saint,
All who survived current ignominy.
Places of learning grew in North and South,
Where themes made music for all ears to hear;
With tune of Hopkinson chorused from mouth
All *Hallelujah!* rendered without fear.

Above the freedom won by force so far
America in culture rose to star.

Colonial Grace of Faith

Wars of humanity put faith to test
That more than for the flesh the mind must strive;
When battles of the brain and body rest,
The soul to heaven lifts and stays alive.
Catholics Roman and Anglican withstood
The trial broken off episcopates;
Ministers Protestant still wore the hood
That global bishopric anticipates.
Vermont's Green Mountain Boys helped all to see
How Ethan Allen oracled the throng;
Religion for republic was kept free
To make all future faith like reason strong.

A revolution firms fraternity,
While grace of God confirms eternity.

Colonial Upper Class

The style of home shaped the colonial class
Wherein people mirrored Court of St. James;
Puritanism declined to the mass,
While wealth castled gallants and chosen dames.
Like hospitality that Boston ruled
Society in Williamsburg soared high;
With trade of rum, codfish, and slaves unschooled
Both North and South contended for the sky.
The History of the Dividing Line
By Byrd describes the haves and the have-nots;
Words of Ben Franklin, now deemed as divine,
Gunned all land luxury with voice-armed shots.

Who were or were not class in colonies
Were judged by mansions owned by the grandees.

Colonial Dawn of Reform

Estates of Loyalists to Patriots passed
With confiscation making owners new;
As freedom for all people so was classed,
Equality of all was in the brew.
The rights of liberty by Constitution
Encouraged abolition of black slaves;
Some states would ban this social institution,
Though their future they might bury in graves.
People and land the Colonies made free
With Rights as Declaration had confirmed;
When blacks with whites were seen equal to be,
Nation would have its premises affirmed.

As States with independence did conform,
The nation for its strength dawned with reform.

The Great Awakening

At Yale Commencement, seventeen twenty-two,
The Reverend Cutler stirred women and men;
Exhorting what for them their faith would do,
He urged, "Let all the people say *Amen!*"
Jonathan Edwards by sermons and script
Spurred Whitefield and Wesley to spread the Word;
Religion by Awakening was gripped
By all the free who word of God had heard.
Past Calvinism, universities
Keep courses of theology alive;
Religion with chosen diversities
Helps all Americans with strength to strive.

Eternal spirit lifts all weight of stress
From who awake to rise with holiness.

Queen Anne's War

In government no cipher was Queen Anne,
The "Mrs. Morley" classed with middle drift;
"Augustan Age" of English she did span
With Addison, Defoe, plus Steele and Swift.
Spanish succession plunged her into war
That with Treaty of Utrecht came to stand;
Her navy had captured all Gibraltar,
Minorca, Argentia and Newfoundland.
When France *la guerre de course* in commerce lost,
The war of navies ended for the Queen;
England, whose sea power had once been tossed,
Now had the greatest that had ever been.

The Queen who saved her nation from disaster
Was termed "a sweet, [a] just [and] boyish master."

English versus the Spanish

Learning from the mistake of Queen Anne's War,
Britain made plans for Georgia to be found;
General James Oglethorpe became the star
Sparked by the Cherokee who gave up ground.
With "War of Jenkin's Ear" in thirty-nine
Hostilities were all renewed with Spain;
Edward Vernon sacked Porto Bello line
And sought to overwhelm the Spanish Main.
When Oglethorpe and Vernon met defeat,
Their troops with term "Americans" were named;
Since they at Bloody Marsh did Spanish meet,
For independence action they are famed.

Since war with Spain ended in seventeen forty-eight,
Founding of Georgia rates James Oglethorpe as great.

Canada versus English in the North

As Queen Anne's War made Canada too weak,
A nation lacking both people and trade,
One force alone gave her the strength to speak,
A trained militia that the crown had paid.
At Nova Scotia, Louisbourg, and Maine
The French Canadians lost all defense;
Then with the forts like Crown Point, Lake Champlain,
Their explorations widened, but with dents.
In North America France met her fate,
As she with Iroquois would Boston burn;
Aix-la-Chapelle treaty of forty-eight
Made England swap conquest with land return.

As Nova Scotia moored English majority,
British deported French hostile minority.

Acadian Deportation

During King George's War they neutral stood,
Firm French Acadians on Fundy Bay;
With peace and British winning shore and wood,
Hardship forbade the "Cajuns" there to stay.
Acadians, more than six thousand, fled
To Canada either by woods or sea;
Like Protestants in France from force they sped
In vastest banishment in history.
Two separate groups at seed may not combine,
As one in peaceful area to flower;
Algeria, Cyprus, and Palestine
Today prove the perimeter of power.

Acadians proved that Americans might be
Subject to Europe and its martial strategy.

Cold War Windings (1747–1755)

The question was "Who was to rule the West?"
France, England, Spain, or the United free?
Plan of Union, Franklin-Hutchinson test,
Faced strategy of English ministry.
Dinwiddie, Sharpe, Shirley with Braddock met,
Who made George Washington an aide-de-camp;
Franklin diplomacy the tactics set
With Conestoga wagons on the ramp.
On way to Fort Duquesne Braddock met doom
At sight of French and sound of Indian whoop;
Soldiers at sundown panicked from the gloom,
As death of Braddock left a scattered group.

When Dunbar for Penn's City left the tents
The P.M.V.* frontier had no defense

*Pennsylvania, Maryland, Virginia.

Seven Years' War (1755–1763)

Braddock's defeat plus French and Indian War
Merged into Seven Years over the world;
In seventeen fifty-eight there rose a star,
A William Pitt who British flag unfurled.
Louisbourg recaptured by Boscawen
And Frontenac by John Bradstreet controlled
Revealed for victory the how and when
George Washington for marching on enrolled.
Wolfe warred Montcalm in seventeen fifty-nine
With quickest victory of history;
In North America France lost its line
With Peace of Paris, seventeen sixty-three.

With Heart of Oak Britain was still a star
Before the dawning of another war.

Triumph and Test

Americans, English, Irish, and Scots
Shared unity in seventeen sixty-three;
With loyalty of proven patriots
They faced the power trial of victory.
Shipbuilders, sailors, fishermen, and gents
Became the freest people in the world;
While biding law, they dashed into its dents,
Like smuggling 'neath the British flag unfurled.
Like Reverend Clap, the president of Yale,
Who studied Mercury with telescope,
The colonists climbed every hill and dale
While Christian faith gave science every hope.

British Americans sought to affirm
The freedom that was theirs they would confirm.

Imperial 1763

Tenure of judges still controlled by crown
In colonies managed minorities;
But those for faith and race Europe held down
Became new-world ruling majorities.
With compromise of seventeen sixty-three
Between control and home self-government
Americans assembled liberty,
Controlling law and taxed constituent.
When George the Third would their freedom impair,
They first expressed loyal expostulation;
Their armed resistance became action fair,
Resulting from indignant agitation.

The Revolution aimed but to preserve and stress
Life, liberty, and the pursuit of happiness.

United Solution of Royal Problems

The ministries of King three problems met—
In West with Natives, fur traders, and land,
In Acts of Trade and Navigation set,
In money for defense with a firm hand.
With law enforcement problem tackled first,
The Pontiac's Rebellion warned off West;
Revenue Act of sixty-four then burst
With taxes to make all defense grow best.
Stamp Act of Parliament in sixty-five
Was more than colonies would tolerate;
Like Sons of Liberty they came alive
To force repeal that made them celebrate.

Like victory political Americans first won,
United opposition the most since then has done.

Townshend Act Crisis Countdown

America was taxed by Townshend Act
On paper, glass, all paint, and India tea;
With benefits to royalty a pact,
Commissioners of Customs set the fee.
Like "Pennsylvania Farmer," Dickenson,
Who twelve letters scripted for federal rights,
Bostonian Sam Adams by exposition
For Sons of Liberty broadened their sights.
First orchestra leader of Revolution
Like Roman Ovid would "stand at the start";
With letter circulating evolution,
Boston Convention staged his leading part.

Convening delegates was deemed extraordinary,
A crisis rulers judged as revolutionary.

Western Woe

Too rapidly Western frontiersmen flew
Like scattered bees searching to build their hives;
Meanwhile the Sons of Liberty all grew
As one to sting the taxing of their lives.
Back country settlers needed government
To battle brutes, horse thieves, and Indian raids;
With *Regulators* nesting discontent,
They fought the levies trooping at their glades.
Battle of Alamance in seventy-one
Ended rebellious War of Regulation;
But encroachment of Indian country won
In seventy-four the Royal Proclamation.

Land speculators welfared by their woe
For independence made Britain their foe.

Pre-Twentieth-Century Mohawks

Mohawks refuse to put their weapons down,
Or end casino gambling of their own;
For Indian affairs spoke Eddie Brown
To voice why from St. Regis all have flown.
Like eagles who to hawks might lose their nests
Their Warrior Society patrols;
They have with New York troopers met all tests,
While tone of gunfire in distance rolls.
U.S. and Canada's officials meet
To silence sounds of rising revolution;
Mohawks on reservation might yet greet
Their own negotiation as solution.

Be it with problem Indian or Russian
May warring now be fought by codiscussion.

Nonimportation Movement

To boycott import of taxed British goods
Became the question of the colonies;
Repeal of Townshend duties cleared no woods
Where radicals made loyalists dead trees.
Replacing soldiers for workmen on strike
Was like shooting the mob with death for two;
This "Boston Massacre" became the pike
That mounted what the royalists would do.
When William Pitt the House of Lords addressed,
He claimed Americans must strive by trade;
If seeking liberty were overstressed,
Their break from Mother Country would be made.

Nonimportation rule, though put to ice,
Firmed colonies to shed British advice.

Prerevolutionary Calm

Of "Boston Massacre" Sam Adams roared,
While colonies prosperity enjoyed;
John Hancock above agitation soared
Like eagle Ben Franklin who peace employed.
New York, Boston, and Philadelphia calmed
Down to "state of insensibility";
So termed one Thomas Jefferson, alarmed,
Who like Sam Adams would have people free.
Governor Hutchinson kept up debate
With Sam on principles of Constitution;
Adams to Greeks and Latins would relate
For causes calmed before a revolution.

No state of peace in life has firmer form
Than that of the quiet before the storm.

Gaspee Grief

When skies are bright with clear and strong starlight
A rising cloud may soar into the air;
Attack on tax cutter on one June night
Thundered the fire of *Gaspee* affair.
Rhode Island patriots who vessel burned
Demanded trial by own community;
To grief for Townshend duty they returned,
Facing the problem of taxes on tea.
Attempt to apprehend who burned *Gaspee*
Persuaded burgesses to organize;
Boosting by Henry, Jefferson, and Lee
Gave to machine of Adams greater size.

First act for freedom that may move with grief
In rallied revolution finds relief.

Shays's Rebellion

Debtors and poor farmers in states increased
With produce, trade, and labor standing still;
When all aid to insurgents was decreased,
Things pushed one Daniel Shays against his will.
At Petersham force of Rebellion broke,
Whence Shays had to Vermont then to escape;
In Paris Jefferson deemed this the stroke,
The lightning of the storm in the landscape.
"Rebellion now and then is a good thing,"
He claimed, to freshen "tree of liberty";
Tyrants and patriots with bleeding bring
More strength to governing authority.

Rebels like Shays aroused total attention
To serve Union by Federals in Convention.

Federal Convention, 1787

Federal Convention, from May to September,
In Penn's Town met in seventeen eighty-seven;
It versed the draft all people will remember,
The Constitution, legal proof of heaven.
Contest defeated "high-toned" government
With choice of elections by votes of states;
Decision championed the Tenth Amendment
That power national with people rates.
Balance of Constitution proved unique
With statesmen like those of Athens and Rome;
Though cracks of imperfection still now creak,
It motors the protection of each home.

Founder of the Republic had one hold—
Ideas of all people each would uphold.

Ratification Rift

Convening Congress of Confederation
Passed Constitution to be ratified;
With a nine-state approval for the nation,
Convention felt all would be gratified.
Federalists and Anti-federalists rift arose
With cleavage between youth and those of age;
As knowledge with more education grows,
Essays of "Publius" calmed down the rage.
From quarter-century tumult that ensued
For colonies with constant revolution
Diversity to unity pursued
The form that shaped the Federal Constitution.

When federal principle found application,
Ratification unified the nation.

First President

Past progress from Mount Vernon to Wall Street,
George Washington peaked as first President;
The mount of problems that he had to meet
Made his control of judgment evident.
With strength of Court Supreme in evidence,
George called on Congress for full consultation;
Advice of people coursed his confidence
To make a central seat for the whole nation.
An eagle stretching space to nest each dove,
George Washington to cabinet conformed;
The Congress that he ruled from branch above
For "State of the Union" he kept informed.

Relations bolstering administration
First President confirmed the faith of nation.

Alexander Hamilton

A. Hamilton, ahead of his own time,
Paternalism matched with laissez-faire;
Like lightning that makes clouds of thunder climb,
He sparked charges that nation had to bear.
Virginians refused taxes for New York;
Nor would plain folks for ruling gentry pay;
One Patrick Henry rose like ruffled stork
Screeching that liberty for flocks must stay.
As Alexander remonstrance so read,
He veered to Jefferson as to a star;
State Secretary turned for light instead
To candle of Virginia lit for war.

The breach divided the slave-holding South
From Northern cities with seaports at mouth.

Thomas Jefferson

With literature, science, and the fine arts
Combined in mind of Thomas Jefferson,
He would for the oppressed divide all parts,
A goal as nonsense judged by Hamilton.
In struggle of control of Constitution
Jefferson fought the favors of finance;
Reports of Hamilton stirred resolution
For organized dissenters to advance.
New York the Jeffersonians "botanized,"
Seeding "Sons of St. Tammany" in field;
Aristocratic faction poetized,
Freneau led opposition not to yield.

Party Republican of Jefferson
With Democrats divided Washington.

John Adams

By Franklin deemed as great, honest, and mad,
John Adams proved as poor Vice-president;
Though best political science he had,
Some lack of leadership was evident.
With frigate *Constitution* stuck on shore,
France cleaved the countries of the Western world;
Russia, Britain, U.S.A., but no more
Marched on their own while flags remained unfurled.
Adams adopted armed neutrality
To protect commerce and respect the flag;
With France in quasi-war formality,
The symbol soared above each foreign rag.

In Philadelphia J. A. hustled for peace
With U.S. Navy surged for safety to increase.

Washington Policy

George Washington sought union, justice, peace
To integrate one nation and one flag;
Past Revolutionary War release,
He would not have union of nation lag.
Fairness on foreign policy he weaned
To protect trades, commerce, and navigation;
While Jefferson and Hamilton careened,
The President primed structure of the nation.
As he foreign and Indian problems faced,
George smoothed all conflicts with tranquillity;
Opposing sides with unity he braced,
Each one to serve with shared equality.

As Washington staged nation to his way,
Two-party system lives like his today.

Washington Doctrine

George Washington's doctrine of isolation
Would cultivate harmonious peace for all;
With faith and justice toward every nation,
He would not as a slave to power fall.
With any portion of the foreign world
Of firmed alliances he would stay clear;
The leader for defense kept flag unfurled
While ready for emergencies to steer.
Interests of Europe have remote relation
To the concerns that in the new world move;
Because of detached distant situation
Her controversies are her own to prove.

Among people who for discordance had the germ
George Washington kept rule that was tranquil but firm.

Franco-American Politics

In seventeen ninety-three all felt for France
A "War of all people against all kings";
French Revolution gave U.S. the chance
To use Neutrality (to) Act for things.
With *Age of Reason* scoffing at the French
Whose "philosophes" defended wealth of land
Tom Paine gave John Tyler the words of bench
That law of Britain had the stronger hand.
Around two poles the nation crystallized—
The British Federalists and Jacobins for France;
Dichotomy a permanence realized
That pros and cons would politics enhance.

While Franco reason would cut government in two,
For Union to endure George Washington stayed true.

Jay's Treaty

Jay's Treaty, signed in seventeen ninety-four,
Built up U.S.-British West Indies trade;
For grounding peace it made secure the floor
For House whose roof of justice could be made.
The contract structured settlements with Spain,
While it evacuated Northwest posts;
Eternal amity, its greatest gain,
Made England and America cohosts.
The Treaty was issue of next campaign
That narrowly made Adams President;
America with unity would reign
With strength that peace of States made evident.

As thoughts of Jay's a Constitution won,
So did the ways of who ruled Washington.

Crucial 1794

Most critical was seventeen ninety-four
For federal U.S.A. experiment;
Outraged by Barbary corsairs and more,
Congress coursed Navy reestablishment.
When Canada would make an Indian state
As product cashing on St. Clair's defeat,
At Fallen Timbers Wayne reversed the fate
While Jay in London made warring retreat.
As twenty years of fighting came to end
With Greenville conference a forest clear,
From War of Independence all would bend
To People whose land ownership was dear.

With "Fifteen Fires" of the States burnt out,
All learned what Independence was about.

States' Rights

When refugees first came to U.S.A.
And in actions of treason some engaged,
Sedition Act forced States to seek the way
For battle of their Rights hence to be waged.
The Federalists Reign of Terror was not real,
As the Republicans had so proclaimed;
The sparks of *habeus corpus* once ideal
With flames like "Fries Rebellion" became famed.
Since Federalists primed those of Revolution,
They led nation as union to secure;
People of States confirmed by Constitution
Chose Jefferson for freedom to make sure.

"That in the fall of laws a loyal man should die,"
States' rights in victory expanded forces high.

Nineteenth Century

Thomas Jefferson, President

Pursuing happy life and liberty
Primed Thomas Jefferson as president;
Believing in perfectibility,
His idealism became evident.
For government he sought freedom from fears
When people with reason associate;
By his address he sought to wipe the tears
Of laborers who earned more than they ate.
Against some federal judges T. J. moved
And would have some like Justice Chase impeached;
Success by trial conservatism proved
That rule of law by nation had been reached.

As strength of Jefferson extended beyond nation,
He proved the power of brilliant administration.

Aaron Burr Conspiracies

Northern Confederacy sought separation
From rule aristocratic of the South;
Conspiracies hence rose within the nation
Like those of Aaron Burr, loyal in mouth.
When Hamilton with leadership in hand
Battled the traitor at the price of death,
The plots of V.P. to break up the land
Proceeded with the maximum of stealth.
Success in Europe with his piracy
Strengthened the Judas who more schemes announced;
The "dark, wicked widespread conspiracy"
Presiding Jefferson firmly denounced.

Conspiracies like Burr's within the nation
Give independence foreign complication.

Embargo Act

As England shot U.S. gunboats to leak
And stopped all vessels her deserters sailed,
She poured three broadsides on the *Chesapeake*
And proved that her impressment had not failed.
Wise Jefferson, the President serene,
For trade had Congress pass Embargo Act;
What for people source of living had been
Now caused them to divide and to react.
The so serene Southern aristocrat
Both Federalists and Tories undermined;
Future Republican or Democrat
His paced equality would seek to find.

While to burn Europe did the mad Napoleon strive,
The flame of liberty Jefferson kept alive.

Drifted Madison Diplomacy

Great statesman for the federal Constitution,
James Madison was politician poor;
Treaty with Erskine by his resolution
Might have avoided second British war.
Without his lead Congress passed Macon's Bill
For intertrade between Britain and France;
As merchant tonnage then rose up the hill,
West Florida J. M. aimed to advance.
Winter of eighteen-twelve made England freeze,
Who hoped for heat of act by its repeal;
Too late did Castlereagh reach from the squeeze
That for Congress tightened war bells to peel.

Leaders who on the sea of power drift
May waves of peace by a lost hour shift.

Rising 1812 War Fever

The pros and cons for war with fever burned
From bites of hawks saving their nests of land;
While "British yoke" on Stars and Stripes was spurned,
The Indian question forced the strength of hand.
Tecumseh and Tenskwatawa, the twins,
Forced a confederacy for trade defense;
At Tippecanoe they sought to fight the sins
That made presence of white men an offense.
Events made patriots grow keen for war
To absorb Canada and Indian whoop;
They would one nation make to be the star
To shine above the European loop.

New England versus South the problems wrought
For which the War of eighteen-twelve was fought.

Aggressive Push to War of 1812

From Canada when Hull's invasion failed
Americans returned for homes to hold;
British Java, Guerriere, and Peacock sailed
Away from U.S.A. grown strong and bold.
Though naval victories were slight to spell,
Battle of Thames by riflemen was won;
When Fort Niagara to British fell,
Troops of Hamilton and Wilkinson seemed done.
Defensive warfare by the English waged
Cleared Canada of troops of U.S.A.;
But future turn of action hence was staged
For true Americans to lead the way.

With phase aggressive having wrought offense,
The War of 1812 pursued defense.

Defensive War of 1812

Niagara, Champlain, New Orleans fought
On to "Macddonough's Victory" for States;
But Robert Rose and George Cockburn then wrought
Defeat of Washington burned to its gates.
With generals killed at the "dawn's early light,"
Winning at Chesapeake made U.S. strong;
Star Spangled Banner flying through the night
Stirred Francis Key to write the nation's song.
Brave Andrew Jackson, who had "Red Sticks" crushed,
At New Orleans brought British to defeat;
From men on parapet lost English rushed,
Withdrawing to transports in full retreat.

The War of 1812 ended its story
With "Second War of Independence" glory.

Union in Peace

New England fever to secede cooled down
While men from Plattsburg promised real reprieve;
The Duke of Wellington warned British crown
That war with U.S.A. would nil achieve.
One Christmas Eve both signed Treaty of Ghent
For the conclusion of hostilities;
Commission organized for peace was bent
On restoring the prewar boundaries.
The futile conflict did help the two nations,
As parent and a child exchange respect;
With independence in future relations,
America to peace would world direct.

As freedom was the force of new world revolution,
It unified the course for peace and Constitution.

Era of Good Feelings

Weary of parties and sections in strife,
America, one nation, grew in strength;
To rival interests statesmen gave life
And to theories of states rights added length.
Era of Good Feelings was well defined
By leaders John Calhoun and Henry Clay;
Roads and canals that could Republic bind
Built for "American System" its highway.
By foot, horseback, or wagon people moved
On routes still leading from the East to West;
Traffic the once Creek nation so improved,
It made all minds exchange their very best.

When more than War for Independence has been won,
No joy is greater than to make the nation one.

Warring Wind-Blown Missouri Compromise

A storm rising to crack over the West
Thundered to panic those who moved from East;
Public Land Act for people did its best,
But hard times darkened sunshine to its least.
Lightning meanwhile was striking North and South,
Crashing along old Mason-Dixon line;
With argument of slavery in mouth,
Lions of Congress would freedom define.
Missouri Compromise did crisis spell
While with its print it gave a future view;
When Jefferson at night saw "fire bell,"
As "knell of Union" he thought it would do.

John Quincy Adams warned in his recording column
This was "a title page to a great tragic volume."

Anglo-American Modifications

Uneasy postwar minds as one may flow
By statespeople who do the most for peace;
Lord Castlereagh, Madison, and Monroe
From wars sought international release.
Rush-Bagot agreement bound naval force
To four single-gun vessels on the Lakes;
But underflowing friendliness was course
For settlement to equalize the stakes.
When Jackson had arrested Seminoles
And forced secession of all lands of Spain,
British-Americans raised power poles
While the United States vaunted in vain.

Firmness of Castlereagh in all emergency
Forced Anglo-New World peace as living policy.

Monroe Doctrine

Farm houses built with classic colonnades
Templed the base of U.S. education;
Struggle for independence rolled up shades
To give America new light as nation.
Monroe Doctrine for history declared
New World no colony of Europe's power;
System political would not be shared,
Securing peace and safety for the hour.
With other colonies not interfered,
The States avoided European war;
When principles of doctrine thus appeared,
It for all policy became the star.

National consciousness by Monroe built
Keeps independence firm at base and hilt.

President John Quincy Adams

Elected president in eighteen twenty-four,
John Q. Adams with love of country burned;
Social compact to waken nation more,
Those who "slumber in indolence," he spurned.
He would increase Navy and build more roads
For country centered in strong Washington;
Latin America he freed from goads
By delegates who knew what should be done.
Recommendations Adams gave to nation
Were years later adopted as the law;
Chautauqua, forums, adult education
All moved to vision he by genius saw.

"Jefferson-still-surv-," words of final speech,
Voiced Adams with his Independence reach.

Presidential Election, 1828

The 1828 election smelled
With frontier brawls and most absurd of lies;
But people classed in states the victory spelled
With personality that wealth defies.
Hunters of South and backwoods farmers moved
For Jackson who for their own glory ran;
Against promotions of White House they proved
That Andrew J. was their own sort of man.
John Quincy Adams, thus by country spurned
By people he had served so faithfully,
To silence of integrity returned,
Feeling "The whole wide world abandoned thee."

Election proved for J. Q. A. instead
That best of his career lay just ahead.

Jacksonian Democratic Rule

Great figures parceled politics of nation—
Clay, Adams, Webster, Van Buren, Calhoun;
A giant standing high in each relation,
One Andrew Jackson was the greatest boon.
Jacksonian structure disunion opposed,
But leveled not with people red or black;
Rough-hewn "Old Hickory" as ruler posed
Beyond log cabin that had birthed his track.
As he to White House rode on saddle horse,
Another revolution came to view;
With masses and aristocrats in course,
His iron constitution led him through.

With slight knowledge of books for race at hand,
Jackson to rising nation gave command.

Cabinet Battles, 1830–1831

Spoils system gave supporters their demands,
Who, like Calhoun, maneuvered President,
Scandal of Peggy Eaton shook the stands
Of those who thought secession evident.
Each man of cabinet fought for himself,
Forcing Martin Van Buren to resign;
With all the small fry then put on the shelf,
Andrew Jackson could reconstruct design.
With cabinet distinguished made—and strong—
With the "Eaton Malaria" full cured—
With "Calhoun the Traitor" wiped out for wrong—
Jackson for second term was well assured.

U.S. the best of A. J. has observed
Is that the Federal union he preserved.

Tariff of Abominations

Pro-Jackson congressmen passed a new bill
With higher duties on material raw;
This stirred a local turmoil on the Hill
That for Union of States fomented flaw.
Southern plunder of capital of North
Led to the doctrine of nullification;
Each State as Sovereign would hence move forth
For privileges beyond the law of nation.
Like a noble Roman Calhoun stood firm
On his conceptions of land liberty;
Products of slave labor he would confirm
To owners who protected blacks as free.

"Tariff-abominations" that remained
Let South to seek how West for all refrained.

Jackson versus the Bank

The Democratic party Jackson formed,
While the Republicans shaped liberty;
Battle of President then became normed
As Bank of U.S. powered it to be.
When Clay rechartered bill for B.U.S.,
Veto of President darkened the star;
Biddle like moonlight rising from the stress
Revealed the rays of a financial war.
Strife of Jackson with bank was an ideal
That dream of Boston Tea Party still sparked;
Hope led people to sail to the New Deal
But on the roughened sea was still embarked.

When bank dropped Philadelphia as glade,
Financial capital it New York made.

Eternally Andrew Jackson

Among greatest of presidents most real
Wise Andrew Jackson rates for all of time;
For all of people he had sound appeal
With chivalry approaching the sublime.
His forthrightness and lack of compromise
Were of a lion protecting his den;
To end disruption he proved always wise
Despite mistakes of choosing hunting men.
When he passed on, the ground began to swell
With slavery problems as the rising spring;
His great appeal might have relieved the quell
And proved how much he was a natural king.

For character and common sense as wings
Of eagle Andrew Jackson nation sings

1837 Panic

Van Buren, a "Little Magician" named,
As President was wise and dignified;
With the best men of Whigs already famed,
To strengthen Union he pursued and tried.
Beneath progressing boom of wealth of nation
Overextended credit made a void;
As banks promoted further speculation,
A crisis loomed that nothing could avoid.
Like bud of rose that promises to bloom
With petals crackling for release from rain,
Congress with treasury notes weathered the doom
With debt of country as its lasting gain.

Though President may know basis of all progression,
He must succumb to woe in midst of a depression.

Log Cabin Campaign

The lumberjacks, farmers, and Cajuns shocked
By White House (Caesar's Palace under Van),
With death of voted Harrison then rocked,
For "Tippecanoe and Tyler too" all ran.
Warfare opened between Tyler and Clay
When President killed bill for a new bank;
Between the Whigs and West fermented fray
Because wood owners gave loggers no rank.
The eighteen-forty Log Cabin campaign
Is basest contest of our history;
Patronage to "get out the vote" to gain
Was but log-cabin demagoguery.

As lust for office was a rising fog,
The wrath divine revealed each cabin's log.

Canadian Blow-up

The British North America was known
Like Canada, subject to rule of crown;
Frustration of the pioneers had grown
Like that of rising hopes that are held down.
People, quashed by the ruling oligarchy,
Led by genteel Louis J. Papineau,
Seeking a fair deal free of monarchy,
Caused the explosion in Ontario.
When volunteers sank down the *Caroline,*
Van Buren sought shores of diplomacy;
Thus Canada's rebellion docked to line
Colonials free from all autocracy.

Outcome to blow-up led nations to leaven
To North American Act of sixty-seven.

American Self-Discovery

The eighteen-hundred's crucial generation
Patterned what all Americans would be;
Two parties after storm of nullification
To preserve Union pledged their loyalty.
Forbearance with the other was their mode
In bustling age when each would climb a tree;
Beyond forest of work through fields they rode
Of Emerson, Whitman, Longfellow, Lee.
Once past cesspools the watercloset came
To houses still heated by fireplace;
Crude U.S.A. with culture built its frame,
A government of freedom with all grace.

America is land of dream come true,
Where people find and live all they can do.

Nineteenth Century by Land and Sea

The pioneers for best moved to the West
To prairies of tough sod, timber, and grain;
Railways, canals, and roads helped pass the test
Like that of New York for Northwest to gain.
Canals of "portage system" cities tied
That then by railroad their connection made;
On waters shipbuilders new vessels tried
As docks at Liverpool improved in grade.
U.S. ships sharply built and canvassed white
Shamed English dirty vessels, great black tubs;
As Black Bull Line rushed captains into night,
The Western Ocean gave to wheels new hubs.

As sails American quickened the reach of nation,
The dream of Independence eased flow of immigration.

Daniel Webster

Debate progressed for public land in West
And how it welded to the Constitution;
Whether the North or South as friend was best
Made Daniel Webster speak with resolution.
While Union lasts, he said, prospects spread out
To where one cannot "penetrate the veil";
When curtains rise where people move about,
Union and Liberty as one prevail.
Fraternal blood by civil feud made drenched
Must not make view of strength irreparable;
One truth above the curtain still is wrenched—
"Liberty and Union—one and inseparable."

Webster to Jackson gave the words conserved—
"Our Federal Union—it must be preserved."

Intellectual Devotion to Democracy

One fringe of people culture in New York
Cheered Cooper and Irving as U.S. choice;
Poets for wine of words loosened the cork
De Ponte poured for the opera to voice.
For intellects word-makers pressed the core
With periodicals and ministrel show;
Unknown for *Moby Dick,* Melville did more
As a customs inspector on the know.
Bryant supported strikes with *Evening Post*—
Hawthorne about campaigns with fiction wrote—
Clerkship in New York Customs House was most
That Democrats to writers gave to note.

To hotchpot deeds Walt Whitman gave his best,
While party peers put *Leaves of Grass* to rest.

Rising American Art

Be it Sully, Bryant, Durand, or Cole,
Artist American reflected scenes;
Art Union urged the members as a whole
To portray all people as kings and queens.
New York the center of fine arts became
From limn of landscape to the house design;
With genius like Downing of White House fame,
Country estates roofed every cultural line.
America of nineteenth century
Astonished foreigners with its fine things;
It proved that freedom to the arts can be
What gives to mediocrity new wings.

As culture coursed from uninformity,
U.S. with arts pursued conformity.

Cotton Royalty

Cotton in U.S. South became the king,
Black slavery being bulwark of throne;
With sugar and tobacco in the ring,
Disputes were stabbed as in "affray" of Cone.
Conditions led to rise of mountain men,
"Hilbillies" drifting from all parts of South;
Nondependent hunters and fishermen,
They whiskied cotton workers by the mouth.
The Southern white gentry counted as few,
And yeomen farmers became "poor white trash";
Professional careers could nothing do,
While owners of plantations whipped the lash.

While industry in North spread with democracy,
Cotton planting in South bred aristocracy.

Slavery State

Cotton plantations spread with hands of slaves,
Who had been bought in Africa from blacks;
From home bondage, preferring New Land graves,
Negroes sought U.S. life with all its cracks.
Since blacks were not equal to whites in nation,
Some hence like Nat Turner stirred insurrection;
Schemes rose for gradual emancipation
From division of race, an imperfection.
Antislavery and procold war was waged
Between white extremists of both on rise;
With failure of emancipation staged,
All lost the peaceful way of compromise.

For the achievement of emancipation
The conflict rose, the worst within the nation.

American Cavalier Literature

The Cavaliers of South, owners of slaves,
Shopkeepers and artists of North despised;
With libraries empty like hidden caves,
They naught of any literature realized.
As abolition agitation rose,
Masters of South decided what to do;
Lee, Jackson, Johnston, Hill, and Moury froze
The written heat of Dew and George Fitzhugh.
Cavaliers of Virginia set the pace
For South to imitate Scott's *Ivanhoe;*
With style of romance as their holy grace,
They tuned with Poe while singing "Old Black Joe."

Like *The Impending Crisis* Helper wrote,
The South its future chivalry would note.

Southern Science and Faith

While Audubon searched quadrupeds and birds,
Matthew Maury charted the ocean breeze;
When scientists made sea safe for the herds,
They faced the "old fields" and their cultural squeeze.
Like daisies forced by roses from the ground
Gardened by hands gilded by owner's gold,
The blacks of South only as slaves could round
For digging what kept earth within its hold.
Proslavery South its Bible faith increased
With evangelical meetings in camp;
Since "spirituals" their emotions released,
They gave their morals a religious stamp.

As people of the world moved for emancipation,
Science and faith for South grooved unity with nation.

American Cultural Charge

America in nineteenth century grew
With heart and mind extending people care;
The rifle of the brain shot out the spew
That clogs the force of strength of those who dare.
The Yankees to New York flew and beyond
With arts and crafts to lift the common roof;
"Coming of Christ" became their bond, a pond
That would like crossing oceans give them proof.
To help the deaf, the blind, and those unknown
Men addressed women as their equal friends;
Like winds that from the voice of God have flown,
"Isms" of faith gave culture open ends.

For a utopia where all are strong and free,
America the most and best has proved to be.

Antislavery Movers

A worldawakening humanity
Arose with abolition as a power;
As prayer will silence most profanity,
Freedom gave slave holders their fading hour.
Reformers—Graham, The Tappans, and Weld—
Demanded unquestioned emancipation;
Poets the brave like Wright and Whittier held
The torch of verse for lighting of the nation.
Phillips, Sumner, Grimkés, and Garrison
Spoke as members of family of minds;
Romance by Hawthorne made each ounce a ton,
Weighing community to scale all kinds.

As Greeley and Evans defined equality,
It was alien with indivisibility.

New England Renaissance

Essay on Nature was the opening key
To door of culture room of U.S.A.;
What was transcendental then proved to be
For human nature its divining way.
"Lay preacher of the world," Emerson rose
With *Little Men* and *Women* Alcott found;
From Dickinson, Thoreau, and Hawthorne flows
What by Longfellow poetry is bound.
For vision Harding and Stuart used paint
To show what Horatio and Powers stoned;
Crawford's Orpheus and Story's "Cleo" saint
By *Marble Faun* of Hawthorne were enthroned.

New England Renaissance gardened at home
The genius that the artists dug in Rome.

Public Education

Free public schools in States were slow to grow
At whip of well-to-do who paid the tax;
But as more studies helped young more to know,
The opposition then had to relax.
By eighteen-fifty schools for all were free
With teachers trained for basic education;
At certain age all children had to be
Absorbed in classics and the books of nation.
Grade classes spread to universities
For law, theology, science, and arts;
This learning welded walls of libraries
That to newspapers loaned some of their parts.

As independence grew within the nation,
Its strongest social gem was education.

Seeding American Science

Ideas of science that old Europe hatched
Were bred in common life of U.S.A.;
Reality with abstraction was matched
By bending arts in the American way.
All electricity Franklin researched
Joseph Henry to know currents induced;
What in electromagnet had been perched
The energy of spiral coil produced.
Machine-tools, rubbers, pistols, clothes, and rakes
Made tide of inventions rise ever high;
On lyceum platforms were seeded stakes
To foster faith while knowing stars of sky.

What ancient world for science theorized
In young America was semenized.

Mountainy Men

Young eagles seeking nests of greater size
Searched land of Oregon for base near sea;
Trading "hide droghers" made them realize
That trip by Rocky Mountains had to be.
Land-trailing immigrants met "mountainy men"
Who guarded them on surface of Great Plains;
Redskins and buffalos within the den
Gave to the "buckskin-clad" their right to gains.
By means of "blowout" reds and whites exchanged
Beaver "banknotes" for alcohol and goods;
When every stream and upland had been ranged
The mountaineers each year took to the woods.

With Indians and mountain men both guides
They gave transcontinental rise two sides.

Oregon Trail

Nathaniel Wyeth trailed to Oregon
By railway, river, steamboat, and the road;
From what he learned frontier folk moved upon
With help of mission groups to bear the load.
Five thousand strong in three years made the trip
With Vancouver Island as U.S. post;
Joint occupation of the ownership
Was made with British who had settled most.
Lord Aberdeen held high the Union Jack,
Extending boundary to Puget Sound;
Canadians to Pacific thus on track
Joined with Americans who West were bound.

Since trappers into Rockies passed Great Plains,
The trail to Oregon for dreams made gains.

Lone Star Republic

Louisianans learned of Mexico
From Texas, spreading province of frontier;
Settlers, who would to land of missions go,
In new Republic had both pride and fear.
Good Mexicans could not swashbucklers be,
Who would as independent nation grow;
From monarchy Texas was hence made free
By Santa Annans after Alamo.
Lone Star Republic by Congress devised
Blew to the North a wind of revolution;
Annexing free state would have compromised
The ones who hailed for slaves by Constitution.

Politicals put all storming to rest
While planters crossed Sabine new life to test.

Wilmot Proviso

That neither slavery should still exist—
Nor forced involuntary servitude,
Wilmot Proviso would have all resist
The loss of racial freedom attitude.
Farmers of North, croppers of liberty,
Stayed free, defended by Seward and Chase;
But extremists of South with property
Developed "slave power" over black race.
Like those tyrants who had Christ crucified
In depth of darkness just before the morn,
American Union on force relied
With which the cross of war tensions was worn.

That all who earned their way should on the land be free
Wilmot exposed the ray of storm about to be.

Gold-Rushed Compromise

In California gold sparked the sand
That piled for her admission as free state;
Both sound and fury rose to shake the land
That threatened North and South to separate.
As sweethearts swimming in a lake of love
Might strike each other when about to sink,
The sight of heaven shook all from above
With compromise that saved them at the brink.
The fugitive slave bill made storm to rise
With problem of Utah and Mexico;
The Congress once again roofed compromise
That beyond 1850 hoped to grow.

Reactionaries and the radicals alive
With tongue of gold of young for unity must strive.

Cuban Unrest

After "Manifest Destiny" of Pierce,
For purchase of Cuba Spain had contempt;
Unrest in island then became so fierce
That annexation might prove worst attempt.
"The Ostend Manifesto" set the pace
For Cuban problem of U.S. and Spain;
It claimed that Union would not future face
Without the island as one purchased gain.
Statement in *New York Herald* gave the "scoop"
That fired fury both home and abroad;
Madrid would prove that it needed no coop
That might be bought and sold like any broad.

All young America of nineteenth century
Viewed Latin nation flare as one flick of the free.

"Young America"

Sparked nineteenth century lightened the sky,
As hope like electricity arose;
With automata all directed by,
"Love, study, and be happy" glowed the prose.
With industry, music, all sports, and arts
In most productive time of Longfellow
All young America booked at its starts
Hawthorne, Emerson, Whittier, and Stowe.
"Manifest Destiny" of Pierce-Marcy
That had "The Ostend Manifesto" scooped
Made question of Cuban democracy
To reading young a line that might be looped.

When "Young America" as group was put to freeze,
It breezed democracy to movements overseas.

Dred Scott

Question of being slaves heated to broil
When one in Illinois claimed to be free;
Dred Scott as resident of the free soil
Fought Court Supreme but won no liberty.
Decision of judgers had triple slate:
Blacks were not citizens of U.S.A.—
Protection was for residents of state—
Scott still was property by legal say.
Sanctions of slaveholding made national
Led to the slave-state versus free-state fight;
Lecompton constitution rational
Made Congress judge proslavery as right.

Dred Scott exemplifies what each state gave
For freedom of the slave from birth to grave.

Lincoln-Douglas Debate

For Senate Abe with Douglas voiced debate,
While shirt-sleeved farmers "Hail Columbia" sang.
Might slavery with territory rate?
The talks with tones of Freeport Doctrine rang.
Though Douglas did his re-election win,
Lincoln in Quincy speech showed what was wrong:
All slavery is morally a sin
When sale makes self to someone else belong.
Replying Senator could not resist
Approving free and slave states both, however;
Admitting thus that slavery must exist,
Douglas for Lincoln timed it as "forever."

Debated words made rise the issue of the land
That house against itself divided cannot stand.

African Slave Trade

The lower South new territory sought
Where slaves from Africa owners would drag;
Traffic in human flesh the pirates wrought
In ships protected by American flag.
Hundreds of thousands blacks reached U.S.A.
While South sought land of Spain and Mexico;
As sparrows with eagles in forest stay,
Hunters sought how pursuit of game would go.
Central America viewed Uncle Sam
As an imperialist of strong intrigue;
Outlawing slavery would help to ram
The trade that made the leader of the league.

The African Slave Trade made clear to more
Divisions that would lead to Civil War.

1860 Election

Election of Sixty sponsored the war,
As with campaign the Union was at stake;
Booth bitterness none wanted any more,
While hanging of John Brown a saint would make.
Torchlight parades and ringing of the bell
Made Lincoln President by people's vote;
But politics stirred slavery to spell
How future poets would the nation quote.
On Christmas Eve South Carolina passed
What South had all pursued as "purple dream";
Their Declaration would an empire cast,
Pooled by African slavery in stream.

Secessionists in tide of John Brown chose to toss
On to gallows as Christ had risen with the Cross.

Cotton States Secession

Seven of South formed the Confederate States,
That would in world another nation be;
This new America had separate gates
Opened to blacks only for slavery.
By Constitution this Confederacy
Declared Negro unequal to the white;
Slave ownership within democracy
They claimed to be a natural moral right.
The cotton states for independence yearned,
A need prevailing over slavery;
By the secession they declared they learned
That war would put to test their bravery.

The South was yet to know it had to trod
Within one nation free and under God.

Border States Contest

By law Lincoln vowed that Union of States
He would protect, preserve, and hence defend;
Confederate officers who gunned the gates
Fired on flag to prove they would contend.
Twenty-three of the states by Union stood,
While with eleven of the South some parched;
Like heat that sparks to burn bound brotherhood
From secession to rebellion they marched.
'Ginia, Carolinas, Kentuck', and Tennessee
In making choice of sides were agonized;
All that made border states contest would be
Efforts that their ideals be recognized.

As the clashing of clouds will crash the view of star,
Attempts to dice with dream brought on the Civil War.

Presidential Cabinets

Lincoln and Davis cabinets contained
Like leaders of perverse and scattered minds;
Experience of Southerner retained
For brain of Abe some strength of many kinds.
Confederate congress lacked the harmony
That work and politics for rule combine;
But dignity and magnanimity
Marked words that Union leader would define.
While Davis made appeal to class and hate
That would the states for slavery divide,
The railsplitter piled logs of tact to fate
That war for strength of Union might provide.

Above both cabinets Lincoln reserved
That unity of nation be preserved.

American Fraternal War

Confederacy by Lincoln realized
Would have Union forever split in two;
For unity the President devised
What for fraternal peace he had to do.
The North and South were two brothers at war
With problems of destroying slavery;
Their parent Abraham embraced both for
"Union forever" with firm bravery.
Vision of Lincoln common people shared
As he proclaimed to end Confederacy;
For future U.S.A. the plans he bared
How to approach global democracy.

A family at home may have to fight
To help the neighbors live by what is right.

One Army for One Nation

In Northern army politicians ranked
To give for war a single country stake;
The Southerners on full conscription banked
With leadership for battle on the make.
Hills, Johnstons, Beauregard, Jackson, and Lee
Were officers of the Confederacy;
McClellan, Sherman, Grant were the top three
Who fought for Union of democracy.
Each side cared naught for pomp nor circumstance,
While all suffered great loss and punishment;
Though army for each nation lacked romance,
The soldiers fell for separate government.

When unity of blue and gray was done,
Two armies joined to make the country one.

Bull Run

Union blockade and Mississippi split
Stirred the Confederacy from timed-out hour;
Abraham Lincoln at the top of it
Kept mind and character of ruling power.
People and press of North for action spun,
And with Lincoln "On to Richmond" they cried;
On July twenty-first near stream Bull Run
Two armies clashed, ill-trained on either side.
"Stone Wall" of Jackson made Union retreat,
But Abe through bitter hour never flinched;
He had the faith that North could South defeat
When proper preparation had been clinched.

While South with self-applause shined its own star,
Union prepared its cause for a long war.

Civil War Tactics

Defending infantry (in double line)
Fired from kneeling posture or erect;
Attacking troops with swords of brightest shine
To beat of drum made forward march direct.
Shouting *Hurrah!*, the boys in blue advanced
While those in gray shrilled back with rebel yell;
With massed artillery for defense chanced,
On Malvern Hill they gained heaven through hell.
With armor ironclad on naval side,
Defense gained strength with submarine and mine;
Rails and balloons on land carried the tide
Beyond what friction did to undermine.

Though moments of combat dealt infantry with death,
Intervals gave contact fraternal voice of breath.

Trent Crisis

From Canada and Britain no support
Lifted the hopes of either South or North;
Blockading and seceding coast and port,
Dividing hand of Lincoln ventured forth.
Hostilities crashed with the *Trent* affair,
When two envoys by Charles Wilkes were confined;
The shouts of war that thundered in the air
The President made light with yield of mind.
Trent episode revealed which clouds had smashed
Since British had declared neutrality;
As reinforcements in Quebec were cashed,
The air was brightened with equality.

A crisis may be just the threat of storm
That stirs contention to a peaceful norm.

Crucial 1862

McClellan, sharp of method and detail,
Army of the Potomac organized;
He felt restraint of soldiers could not fail,
As the offensive war was recognized.
Republicans as Radicals arose
As superpatriots of hate and zeal;
When sail to Farragut the many chose,
Confederacy prepared to break its deal.
In Western theater the action began,
Intoned at Prestonburg and at Mill Springs;
His General War Order then Lincoln ran
That would for eagle forces strengthen wings.

Union in sixty-two, though unprepared,
To rush a War for conquering South it dared.

Ulysses S. Grant

Fort Donelson battle proved U. S. Grant
Initialed with the moral strength of North;
With *U*nconditional *Surrender* chant
He restored faith of Union to go forth.
Battle of Shiloh, Pittsburg Landing, proved
How steadfast General kept cool his sights;
Counterattacking, he to victory moved,
Defended by Lincoln with words: "he fights."
Halleck and Farragut reviewed the role
The U.S. at Vicksburg would well have played;
With Mississippi 'neath Union control,
The voice and hand of Grant new strength portrayed.

As when at sundown shines most brilliant the first star,
So light of Grant defines how generals view a war.

Sea Strength

U.S. blockading squadron squeezed the coast
With paddlewheelers, tug and ferry boats;
Bases on coastline made the North a host
With Navy in control of all the floats.
Runners of South, stealing in dark of moon,
Cargoed with arms and vast consumer goods;
But blockade running proved to be no boon,
As they from ocean sailed rivers to woods.
Confederacy had no ally on sea
As on the Mississippi it was squeezed;
Grant, Sherman, and Thomas would prove to be
The conquerors of storms oceans had breezed.

Since no navy has won alone a strife of nation,
The Civil War proved strength of skillful combination.

Presummer 1862

On the peninsula twixt James and York
The rivers led campaign of South and North;
Army of Potomac with Old Point cork
With sour battle could quench nothing forth.
Johnston with McClellan at Fair Oaks clashed,
While Jackson down the Shenandoah swept;
Actions of Seven Day's Battles then crashed
On wheatfields that the winning Union kept.
Lee in July to Richmond then withdrew,
While Army of Potomac remained safe;
At Harrison's Landing with guns all knew
That Lee would not hence let McClellan strafe.

Conduct of War Committee ordered Army to be
Escorted by Navy to retire at sea.

Summer 1862

One last happy summer the South enjoyed,
Who had a leader found in R. E. Lee;
The master and Jeff Davis charm employed
For loyalty of the Confederacy.
For Lincoln patriots rallied to sing
New words that *John Brown's Body* made them lift;
But bells struck at Manassus tolled to ring
That nation to disunion hence would drift.
With purpose resolute and vision pure,
Abe ordered McClellan command of field;
Lee's crossing the Potomac made it sure
That will to strengthen Union would not yield.

Fifth of September 1862
Forced U.S.A. to what it had to do.

New Republican Party

How could head-on collision time prevent,
Since South would not to slavery give up?
They silenced Sumner whom by stick they bent,
Who had been "Black Republican's" loud pup.
"Jayhawkers" fought Tigers and Kickapoos
While free-staters like crusaders poured in;
John Brown with Pottawotami gave clews
That contents would the Civil War begin.
"Free soil, free speech and Fremont" was the call,
While slavery remained the real issue;
Leaders of South leaned on the lynching stall,
While keeping James Buchanan clear in view.

As leaders from their voters gain more length,
Their differences likewise gather more strength.

Nullification

South Carolina conked the tariff act
As null and void and not binding the State;
But President proclaimed the law a fact
By which all people unify and rate.
As doctrine is detailed in proclamation,
(Each State a Union part with many powers),
Secession would break unity of nation
As falling petals kill the life of flowers.
That Jackson's stem had made the Union strong
South Carolina convention revealed;
The State, with Congress now blooming along,
Nullification ordinance repealed.

Behind the clearing storms of State's accession
Still rose the distant thunder of secession.

Conscription (1862–63)

Either conscription or the loss of war
Made Congress press for service the first act;
Payment of money had the power more
Than patriotism to make men react.
Irish-Americans in riot rose,
Unwilling to abolish slavery;
But those of wealth did the most to oppose
The solidarity of bravery.
Confederate conscription was of class
Fomenting the hatred of white for black;
As price for service spread into the mass
Only amnesty brought deserters back.

The South may well the Civil War had won
If every white man had his duty done.

Equalizing African Americans

As slaves for freedom fled to Union lines
To labor troops and concentration camps,
Le Corps d'Afrique, without any confines,
Gave black soldiers the chance to equal champs.
One Colonel Shaw at Fort Wagner modeled
Americans of African descent;
No matter whom Confederacy coddled,
Both slaves and free blacks were as workers bent.
As General Lee the President implored,
Soldiers of any shade could volunteer;
Of those who this equality explored
Lincoln for global field became the seer.

When move for abolition stirred the nation,
Abe had already termed emancipation.

Politics of Civil War

The ideal tyrant of whom Plato dreamed,
The dictator by law of Constitution,
Lincoln, chief of army and navy beamed
To spark the Union above revolution.
Versed by Emancipation Proclamation,
People both North and South spoke out for peace;
"Heroes" and "Knights" secret organization
Made politics hide plans without release.
Stephens, Brown, Vance, and Bragg of South contrived
Course of Confederacy with discontent;
To all attacks Davis with charm arrived,
No provocation making him relent.

As with his potent power Abe pushed forth,
He scored the warring hour South and North.

Thrusting Campaigns

Battle for Chattanooga opened thrust
Of Hooker, Sherman, and Thomas command;
The rifle-barrels gleaming with full trust
Won Missionary Ridge for their demand.
Union at Red River had its last fall,
Grounded with the defeat at Pleasant Hill;
Sherman then promised Grant to do his all
To win Atlanta with surprise and will.
Four months' campaign was test of war at best
With Johnston's Fabian strategy for fight;
Sherman tricked Hood into attack at crest
To "Head the Fort" while he moved into sight.

Costly campaign for both the South and North,
Atlanta spurred the Union to go forth.

Vicksburg

When Grant forced Pemberton in south Yazoo,
Defeat forced him to Vicksburg from the rear;
Porter with ironclads helped him lead through
One of boldest campaigns of his career.
With Sherman and McPherson, prime of corps,
He made Confederates flee from Champion Hill;
As victory of Haynes Bluff promised more,
Bridge of Big Black River fell to his will.
Lincoln thanked Grant and told him "You were right"
To have defeated Vicksburg by besiege;
The General, genius of soul and sight,
Became responsible for every siege.

The conquest of Vicksburg made all with Abe agree
"The Father of Waters flows unvexed to the sea."

On to Appomattox

From Atlanta Sherman turned to the sea,
Through Georgia marched, and then Savannah won;
Through yellow spot of the Confederacy
He ignored Hood for what had to be done.
"Rock of Chickamauga" (Thomas) met Hood
Whom he stoned with the greatest of defeats;
With fall of Fisher blockade failures stood
As signs of Southern will too weak for beats.
When Four Forks and Petersburg were behind,
White-towelled Lee sought interview with Grant;
Appomattox Court House, a small town kind,
At the McLean home did the scene enchant.

Full-dressed Confederate Lee in doorway paused
To view what the unbuttoned Grant had caused.

Fredericksburg

On forest heights of Fredicksburg Lee stood
To meet stupid Burnside on open ground;
To reach stone wall of Marye's Heights from wood
Six trips made thousands dead to pile a mound.
Horror of Brothers' War with terror moved
All who then fell when struck by shell in brain;
The battle, judged for further contest, proved
That Union army might its strength regain.
Though 1862 gave nation gloom
With little hope for the Confederacy,
Emancipation promised end of doom
If Civil War made one democracy.

"The end of the beginning" was made sure
At Fredericksburg for Union to endure.

On from Chancellorsville

Chancellorsville scened conquest dearly won,
Panic-stricking the Union by surprise;
What General Hooker might by arms have done
Lee did by strategy success devise.
Stonewall Jackson hence Howard's Corps attached
That cavalry found "hanging in the air;"
After two days by the disaster wracked,
For dying hero Lee "wrestled in prayer."
Robert then contemplated further hope
To spring beyond battle of Chancellorsville;
A Pennsylvania won would have him scope
How his promise to South he could fulfill.

Army twixt Chambersburg and Harrisburg
Progressed with stamp of shoes to Gettysburg.

Gettysburg

Great Three-day war on July first began
In little Gettysburg, a quiet town;
Union Ewell and Hill from Hancock ran
To cemetery Hill with Meade in crown.
As barb of limestone Ridge of fishhook shape
Union lost heavily on second day;
Silence on third day then did Culp's Hill drape
Until Lee ordered the advance of gray.
Corps firing at Round Top met Pickett's men
Where Armistead's army was all shot down;
Lee then retired to his Sharpsburg den
From where he felt that future was his own.

Near graves on battlefield of Gettysburg with stress
Lincoln delivered his great Civil War address.

Wilderness Campaign

As Northern strength came close to victory,
It was defied by Wilderness Campaign;
Determined "to hammer continuously,"
From Spottsylvania Grant moved to gain.
From Chickamauga on to Petersburg
By his position he kept Lee pinned down;
Then Franz Sigel, missioned to reach Lynchberg,
With others helped to win the General's crown.
Though warring for nine months continued on
To Battle of the Crate and shared defeat,
From most desperate campaign each had to don
The shreds of losses leading to retreat.

As Lincoln said of Wilderness Campaign,
Each moved nation to rule the whole domain.

1864 Election

After conspiracy breaks every trust,
Only election builds free government;
Political panic would Lincoln bust,
So he to no rebellion gave consent.
Sherman and Grant, forging the civil fray,
Gave fodder for peach movement in the North;
Farragut victory at Mobile Bay
Stirred Buchanan with Navy to sail forth.
Like rider Sheridan, Abe trotted strong
To election of eighteen sixty-four;
Despite confusion of the right and wrong,
His vote though slight still won with who were more.

Panic of Politicians Lincoln bust
As he put the conspiracy to rust.

Lincoln Logo

For new nation conceived in liberty
By braves fourscore and seven years ago
Where all people are born equal and free
Abe spoke on battlefield for civil foe.
Though we may try to consecrate the ground
For those who struggled for their freedom here,
To their unfinished work we all are bound
To cause that by devotion we adhere.
Resolved that dead shall not have died in vain,
This nation, under God, shall have new birth;
Their government the people shall retain,
So freedom shall not perish from the earth.

At Gettysburg Lincoln the words addressed
That U.S.A. for a free world has pressed.

Appomattox Victory

Sun of Confederacy was fading fast
As foreign aid withdrew its lamp of light;
With reelected Lincoln at the mast
The sailing Union gave to South no might.
As strategy of Grant attraction held
And the blockade kept tightening its pinch,
Nothing was left that heart of South upheld,
And its deserters left their given inch.
On April twelfth at laying down of arms
Confederates kissed their flags and laid them down;
Davis of purple dreams softened alarms,
As he in dark turned out of Richmond town.

The night may have the captain most confused,
But battle to surrender he refused.

From Antietam to Emancipation

Between Antietam and Potomac caught,
Lee fought the bloodiest battle of the nation;
The victory gave Lincoln what he sought
For the Emancipation Proclamation.
That slavery must die and nation live
Was covenant that Abe with God had made;
Though Democrats would not the North forgive,
The world would people from the dust upgrade.
Europe the Proclamation hailed with joy
As Christian heroism of the North;
The cause of Union people would employ
As march for human liberty went forth.

As Lincoln spurred freedom in every nation,
All history proclaims emancipation.

Finale of Confederacy

Defeated Lee touched not Davis resolve,
Who summoned Johnston to continue war;
Sherman defeat made all attempts dissolve
With all Confederate losses near and far.
Last battle at Palmetto Ranch was fought
With futile fan of meagre victory;
Then both the Cherokee and Chocktaw sought
Escape like all of Indian history.
Hostilities in the Pacific failed,
Where Yankees burned or scotched those on the trip;
When *Shenandoah* back to England sailed,
Commanders to British surrendered ship.

On sixth of November in eighteen sixty-five
Flag of Confederacy sank down with naught to strive.

Civil Warring Troubled Storms

Monarchy of Napoleon, Mexico,
In Europe kept stretching balance of power;
Ironclad fleet from Nantes and from Bordeaux
Like *Stonewall* fell within the warring hour.
Ships *Florida* and *Alabama* romped
Atlantic to destroy Union at sea;
Like hide-and-seek the would-be captors stomped,
Destroying vessels for Confederacy.
From Canada Confederate soldiers passed
Lake Erie to win *Michigan* by tricks;
The raiders from their breach were timely cast
By orders of brave General John A. Dix.

Conflicts within a town and war at sea
Helped Canada and Union one to be.

Northern Industry

The war helped industry of North to grow
With strength of drive that winds of storm survives;
Union sea power made its service flow
To distant markets reaching foreign lives.
Hundreds of factories made soar the stocks
For woolen and the cotton industries;
Only shipping was struck down to the rocks,
While the sewing and shoe machines raised fees.
When candles the petroleum replaced
New light gave view of size of prairie lands;
Mechanical reaper the farmer graced
To crop King Corn and wheat with motored hands.

"Pike Peak or Bust" did stir the rush to West for gold,
But industry of North gave nation more to hold.

Nineteenth-Century Culture Course

In wartime fifteen colleges were born,
While desks of authors gave life to the pen;
Thoreau, Hawthorne, and Longfellow at morn
Gave light to Emerson to opt the den.
While Walt Whitman wrote sketches of the war,
Lowell with *Papers* made the people smile;
Whittier with loyal verse was like a star
That shined the printed prose of Bryant style.
Timrod, Lanier, and Hayne versed for the South,
For whom Augusta Wilson novel prosed;
They proved Confederate output from the mouth
To be sermons that deaths in war exposed.

Like the Boston statue of Washington by Ball,
Man and Nature by Marsh scriptured the poets all.

Civil War Aftermath

Though "Hang Jeff Davis" was the public cry,
Thirst for revenge was soon well-watered down;
Good citizens as one for peace would try,
Though whites of South still kept their ruling crown.
Southern adversity, though close to death,
Many fine qualities brought to the fore;
While spreading of tobacco stilted breath,
It moved to border states to trade with more.
In arts and letters Southerners had names
Like Barnard, Richardson, and Gildersleeve;
Beyond Confederacy now were the claims
Allegiance could in quality perceive.

As after storm of wind the wheat once more stands high,
All stalks grow equally for the One in the sky.

Lincoln Passage to Eternity

Words *peace, pardon*, and *clemency* all heard
In Washington after the fall of Lee;
With warning dream of what might have occurred,
The play at Ford's Theatre Abe went to see.
At ten thirteen a pistol shot rang out
That made the President slump in his seat;
Sic sempre tyrannis all heard Booth shout,
Who with his gun rushed out to his retreat.
In Tenth Street lodging house upon a bed
Lincoln lifted the clothes with every breath;
With features calm as those that battle led
The saint of patriots passed to his death.

As they recalled the One upon the Cross,
The crowd outside for Lincoln wept their loss.

Post–Civil War Presidential Reconstruction

Freed slaves with silence moved in social place,
While "damyankees" helped South again to rise;
Both North and South for Union paved the pace
That Lincoln for race colonies would size.
Freedman's Bureau of Congress gave relief
That helped all reconstruction to progress;
Each former state Confederate had a chief
Who would from U.S.A. no more digress.
With habeas corpus that all had implored
Johnson declared the "insurrection" dead;
With order, peace, tranquillity restored,
Civil authority tramped with its tread.

Like passing storm that gives the lightning time to strike,
Thunder of President to all sounded alike.

Congressional Action (1866–1868)

Congress committee joint on reconstruction
The Lincoln-Johnson policy opposed;
It would give right of statehood full destruction
That inequality of blacks exposed.
Issue twixt Radicals and President
Rose in campaign of eighteen sixty-six;
With lack of tact by Johnson evident,
Congress for vindication made its fix.
"Peace, pardon and clemency" of Chambrun
Faded to words of force and retaliation;
Had Congress with wisdom of Lincoln run,
Defeated foe would have raced with the nation.

Divided government avoids destruction
When unified by willing reconstruction.

Reconstructing Presidency

Postwar reconstruction tried strong to be,
As white South used Republicans and blacks;
The battled tower stood for unity
Beyond the storm that thundered it with cracks.
Johnson with plan of Lincoln pushed ahead
Civil administration in each state;
But freed ones who sought more than roof and bread
Were made second-class citizens to rate.
With Abe's Emancipation Proclamation
The whites of South would not in life abide;
As they in code railed backward in the nation,
On track of President they would not ride.

What from Lincoln and Johnson it refrained
Congress for reconstruction had retained.

Reconstructed Reconstruction (1867–1875)

State laws of South were purged or modified
By military Reconstruction Act;
Congress by this made "satraps" qualified
To govern as they would an army tract.
New constitutions firmed democracy
For southern states once more to Union turned;
Blacks shaded former white autocracy,
Of whom the most their one-time slaves still spurned.
As reconstructed states moved to disgrace,
The ignorance of freedom nothing gained;
Lacking the education to save face,
Deception was the most the blacks attained.

The worst failing of reconstruction fanned its span
To impeach Johnson and to hood the Ku Klux Klan.

Reconstruction Finale (I)

The Radicals would the government leaven
By making President a Congress chair;
Tenure of Office Act of Sixty-seven
Made leadership sit low for breath of air.
As with passion and prejudice they reached
Beyond the claw of law and valid grounds,
By monstrous charges Johnson they impeached,
Who was acquitted by the saner hounds.
Invisible Empire of the South
Likewise intimidated blacks by guise;
While Grant presided with freedom from mouth,
The Prostate State existed otherwise.

Amnesty Act of Eighteen Seventy-two
Gave whites full privilege to plan and do.

Reconstruction Finale (II)

As Radicals from South moved in retreat,
Carpetbaggers and scalawags fought on;
Weary of reconstruction, Congress heat
Cooled for Conservatives to freeze upon.
While Mississippi forced Ames to resign
For disbanding election-storming blacks,
President of new Senate stood to line
Redeemer governments within its tracks.
Back in Union in eighteen seventy-seven,
Confederate States pursued their own affair;
They reached for their one star in this heaven,
That freedmen's civil rights shine always there.

In viewing episode of reconstruction,
The world admits its conquest of destruction.

Latter-Day Saints

As Church of Jesus Christ Latter-day Saints
With Joseph Smith sought lost tribes to redeem;
Despite polygamy and other taints,
Mormons converted thousands to their team.
Their Moses, Brigham Young, led them to West
Where with the land most desolate they coped;
With system of small farms they dug their best
Corn and potatoes as the gold once hoped.
Community grew in numbers and wealth,
And in the Civil War neutral remained;
By self-respect and comfort without stealth
The happiness of humble folk they gained.

For building commonwealth of English tongue
One saint of spreading world was Brigham Young.

Gilded Age

Like Credit Mobilier and "Whiskey Ring,"
Corrupters defrauded the government;
Pungent persons of power bought each thing
That made purchase of Senate evident.
Pyramid of corruption with wealth rose
To rule what Mark Twain termed the Gilded Age;
Gambling, drinking, and prostitution froze
A nation that once idolized the sage.
As at the common base Longfellow cried
For country with "death-rattle in its throat."
Some would the towers of gold coins deride
And make equality with freedom gloat.

Though eighteen seventies brushed the gleam of bells of gold,
The ringing no dream hushed that would the nation hold.

Nineteenth-Century Euro-American Peace

The strength of Jackson heaved friendship and grace
As he and Great Britain with problems dealt;
With Van Buren and Vaughan face to face,
Restrictions freezing ships were moved to melt.
Averting war was the problem with France
For depredations on the U.S.A.;
Reprisals on French property could lance
As threat that might have fumed into a fray.
United States Navy was unseen force
That paced the peace of nations on the sea;
Thus France and England kept a quiet course
Where sailed America with liberty.

The nineteenth century proved beyond all pretense
That peace depends upon the power of defense.

Nineteenth-Century Latin American Relations

U.S. merchant seamen with Asians fought,
Who plundered *Friendship* and slaughtered the crew;
Yankee Roberts of *Peacock* treaties sought
That cleared Pacific for what Wilkes might do.
Republic Argentine the Falklands claimed
In South Atlantic and Vennet to rule;
When piracy of Captain Duncan flamed,
America from sparking war kept cool.
In Mexico a forging fire burned
With heat of Jackson who for Texas aimed;
The Revolution he had never spurned
Succeeded like the rights that it proclaimed.

Texan rebellion turned every course of the nations,
Twisting to hurt all U.S.-Mexican relations.

Immigration

The immigrants of nineteenth century swelled
To twenty millions seeking the new land;
Like the relief of taxes some compelled,
Freedom for work moved urgently each hand.
Religious and racial riots arose
Like all "American" communities;
Resentment into politics then froze
"Church burners" who bent others to their knees.
With workmen hostile to Irish and blacks,
Whigs pushed the down-and-outs to fatal woe;
"On ice" some fell to drown from "coops" on cracks,
As did one victim Edgar Allan Poe,

Hostility was crossed by growth of nation,
Assimilation of all immigration.

Industrialization

Americans with urban process moved
As in stations of work they spun and wove;
To foreign foresters of globe they proved
That roots of plants strengthen with growth of grove.
Machines to spin and weave cotton and wool
Set pace for factories near waterfalls;
To sell the clock, the chain, the gun, the tool
Rushed Yankee peddlers to all distant malls.
Engines of trade raced with the boot and shoe
Like that of hand and mind that books still bent;
The shoemaker as Senator would do
Or like Wilson become Vice President.

As industry developed cup and wine,
Strength of America reached the divine.

National Partying

Albany Regency example set
For Democratic party to unite;
Led by spoils system, they were bound to get
What for "the people" they believed was right.
Through Union the New Yorker system spread
From stands municipal, federal, and state;
State constitution was the local bread
That to the wine of freedom would relate.
With the communion of Congress and State,
Convention method thus spread nationwide;
With rough and tumble politics in slate,
Ability with ignorance could bide.

Methods political gave voting strength
Like faith that stretched the Federal Union length.

Tenant War

With Rensselaer, the last patron, passed on
The terrorists in Indian garb rebelled;
Berne antirent convention helped to don
The one in forty-six that the State held.
"Let people judge," Walt Whitman hence advised
As Whigs for antirenters old lines crossed;
Defense of Union Democrats had prized
By antislavery was sliced and tossed.
Cornerstone resolution of forty-seven
Was drafted as David D. Field defined;
With code for civil process thus to leaven,
The law reformer led people to bind.

With its hostility uncompromised,
Resolve for freeing slaves was most comprised.

President Hayes?

Historians doubt votes for Presidents
As leaves that cover straws of forest pines;
The cabinet of Hayes was evidence
That harvester the packaged strength defines.
More than others was Rutherford upright,
Who insisted on payment of all debt;
With civil service reforming in sight,
He tried the blend of stronger trees to set.
Political professionals were strong
Who with dislike of righteousness branched firm;
Hence Hayes who would not forest what was wrong
Refused the heaped-up cord of second term.

Democracy that on Congress depends
Must harvest what Hayes honesty contends.

Chester Arthur

Garfield, the President by gun struck down,
Had asked if of Senate he were a clerk;
Struggle of patronage removed his crown,
Shot by an office seeker termed as jerk.
Chester Arthur gave White House royal reign
While he pursued civil service reform;
When he expanded dinner with champagne,
He sought to merit system to conform.
Reformers fought corruption and boss rule
With Appointments based on examination;
As battle with state polls fomented fuel,
The politicians sparked the sights of nation.

Despite critics who would Arthur infest,
Adams *Democracy* deems him as best.

Second Harrison

Late nineteenth century, the *Gilded Age,*
Coined moral miasma of Washington;
Republican Mugwumps conquered the stage
Where Yum-Yumming Cleveland the audience won.
Benjamin Harrison, "Young Tippecanoe,"
Followed the act for greater scene to gain;
As with integrity he all would do,
He opened all curtains with men from Maine;
Though his theme was constructive legislation,
Congress applauded treasury to raid;
While drama of corruption stirred the nation,
Second production at White House was played.

When victor Cleveland once more led the range,
The walls outside shook with the winds of change.

Nineteenth-Century Horizons

The end of nineteenth century upheld
What had transformed during the Civil War;
Railroads, "electrics," and shipping all spelled
The message of all regions near and far.
Transcontinental lines by profit rolled
To open Far West regions unexplored;
Electric streetcars helped cities to hold
By transportation what might have been floored.
Long-distance freight by ships, by sail, or steam,
Captains Courageous led to distant skies;
The San Francisco-Yokohama beam
Gave light to what beyond horizons lies.

Square-riggers officered by U.S.A. Marines
Launched flag American above all of the scenes.

Cowboys and Indians

Invading white settlers with Indians clashed—
Cheyenne, Sioux, Blackfoot, Crow, Arapaho;
Southern Kiowa, Ute, Apache dashed
With horses swift on range to meet the foe.
Defeat of Crazy Horse, Blackfoot, and Crow
Forced Chief Joseph to seek his people's peace;
With the surrender of Geronimo
Warfare of twenty-years scored its release.
While cowboys deemed the Indians good when dead,
Helen Hunt Jackson's book the nation stirred;
When Davis Act gave red man a homestead,
The Five Civilized Tribes joined U.S. herd.

In eighteen-seven Oklahoma state
Made vote of Indians in Union rate.

Cowboy Legend

Raising beef cattle became industry
That gave to the Wild West its final phase;
Palefaces aided by the Cherokee
Crossed Territory for the herds to graze.
The leathered cowboy who the bronco rode
Alert with courage fought rustlers and steers;
Histories of him ancient tales explode,
And ballads of his life sound through the years.
Owen Wister by stories viewed the acts
With glory for cowboys who "grangers" fought;
But the "horse opera" distorts the facts
By which image of the Wild West is wrought.

The Western cowpuncher is dressed as one who chats
With Levi overalls, guns, and "ten-gallon" hats.

Thunders to the West

Each western settlement of U.S.A.
Felt storms of Indian raids and cattle thieves;
Thus North Ohio state cessions gave way
To power colonies to heal all grieves.
Should Congress protect Indians from whites?
How would Confederation roof the land?
Lightning forced townships to huddle for rights
That by the Northwest Ordinance could stand.
The thunder passed without destructive hail,
As lands of West seeded their institution;
Sunshine of liberty would all prevail
For harvest glow of Federal Constitution.

Crackling of clouds often brings blights to sights.
When measured by the heights of Bill of Rights.

Eastern American Indians

With sacred name of Progress Whites progressed,
Expelling all the Reds to take their land;
Indian Removal Act merely expressed
Lean law for liquidation to expand.
Creek, Cherokee, Choctaw, and Chickasaw
Like hunted Hawks were driven from their nest;
From their ancestral trees forced to withdraw,
By "trial of tears" they went from East to West.
As Tuscarora now to Project lose,
Each reservation seeks justice of time;
The greatest Captain of returning crews
Will make their crucifixion be sublime.

As all Whites constantly return to Rome,
Reds will to all America go home.

Lone Star Republic

Sam Houston sought to make Texas a state,
A minor nation next to Mexico;
Though Whigs and Democrats gave this no rate,
President Tyler rushed the cause to grow.
Lone Star Republic was a shining light
Above all politicians' knavery;
With justice for each person in its sight,
It would for rights abolish slavery.
As thunder darkens glimpse of any star
And lightning strikes the air that clouds the sphere,
Battle of Texas shook with sounds of war
That warned the Union that a crash was near.

Twenty-eighth state of nation, Texas proved
America by justice has been moved.

Manifest Destiny

Manifest destiny pursues all ends,
As when a "dark horse" becomes President;
Vox dei made the *populi* all friends
Of Polk who race to West made evident.
The Yanques to California progressed
As Fremont by report of trip inspired;
But President by fears became depressed,
As France and England for the land conspired.
Texas annexation stirred Mexico
To break relations with United States;
As Herrera would not with Slidell go,
It seemed that only war would open gates.

As for Lone Star Republic Polk made claim
Only by battle was destined his aim.

Glorious Conquest

Action annexing Texas brewed for war
As force of Mexico crossed Rio Grande;
For slaves that California wanted more
Protestors like Thoreau were jailed for stand.
Brilliant campaign was led by General Scott
Helped by McClellan, Lee, and U. S. Grant;
Battles at Churusbucco scaled the spot
Where song of victory suppressed each chant.
After blood bath at Molina del Ray
The Halls of Montezuma opened doors;
Guadalupe Hidalgo Treaty way
Corrected surface of what shook the floors,

Conquests with glory might prove to be graves—
Of freedom's "bigger pens to cram with slaves."

Isthmian Canals

Question arose of how canals to cross
To Panama or to Tchuantepee,
Or to Nicaragua without a loss
Of time made by constant controversy.
Clayton-Bullwer Treaty agreement made
That Isthmian canals none would control;
With ambiguity as battle blade,
Americans and Anglos fought patrol.
Bay Islands England to Honduros gave
And Mosquitia to Nicaragua;
But filibustering did naught to save
U.S. hostility, *pedal wa-wa.*

If each isthmus were opened free at first,
Suspicions of Latins would not have burst.

Cuban Unrest

After "Manifest destiny" of Pierce
For purchase of Cuba Spain had contempt;
Unrest in island then became so fierce
That annexation might be worst attempt.
"The Ostend Manifesto" set the pace
For Cuban problem of U.S. and Spain;
It claimed that Union would not future face
Without the island as one purchased gain.
Statement in *New York Herald* gave the "scoop"
That fired fury both home and abroad;
Madrid would prove that it needed no coop
That might be bought and sold like any broad.

All young America of nineteenth century
Viewed Latin nation flare as one flick of the free.

Canadian Ties

Province of Canada with union thrived
Past "Annexation manifesto" brawl;
As reciprocity treaty contrived,
Congress and Parliament settled their quarrel.
Canadian fish, farmed fruit, lumber, and coal
Bought U.S. turpentine, tobacco, rice;
The Lakes, St. Lawrence, and canals made whole
Two nations unified beyond device.
Like heroes in a drama on a stage
After prelude of "oceans of champagne,"
U.S. and Canada solved theme of rage
With that of union clapping every gain.

The nations of New World from shore to shore
All flags unfurled for freedom evermore.

Shipped Nobility

Clipper *Sea Witch* boomed through the Golden Gate,
Proof of new type for California trade;
With tea doubling the ordinary freight,
Strong competition with Britain was made.
In Australia someone discovered gold,
A mine to reach by Black Bull clipper ships;
Champion of the Seas with grace took hold
With majesty that rules challenge of tips.
Like poets transmitting nature to song
The spars and sails balanced mast size and form;
When Yanks, Fijians, and Portuguese sang strong,
They stirred the whales and led them to deform.

As sails for adventure moved with facility
Oarsmen harpooned the whales for shipped mobility.

Prairie Push

Pioneers sought the prairies they could farm
With cultivator, binder, and the plow;
The rising price of wheat was strongest arm
That pushed the farmer to the where and how.
Like crows cawing for way of flock to go
Near sky, the ground, the field, or in between,
For southern route S. Douglas surfed the show
With "popular sovereignty" as sheen.
Once more the slave extension conflict flared
As politicians blazed for growth of power;
Kansas-Nebraska Bill proved what they dared,
Though it might Union blow at any hour.

As hopeful people to the prairies rushed,
The pro and antislavery passions crushed.

Kansas-Nebraska Act

The North and South battled to hold each hill
With Indian territory in between;
Struggle led to Kansas-Nebraska Bill
That raised the seething more than it had been.
As poison within fence of wheatfield grows,
Gospel of ignorance kept all controlled;
Anti-Catholic Know-Nothingness arose
And as American party enrolled.
Passions antislavery flared against pros
Once soothed by the Missouri Compromise;
As gentle breeze into a storming flows,
The strike of radicals cracked up the wise.

While seething over the Kansas-Nebraska Act,
The North resolved to make antislavery a fact.

Eighteen-Nineties Panic

All politics begin to pitch and toss
As from caverns the winds of protest rise;
The Civil War seemed to have blown a loss,
And farmers sought other than western skies.
Populists pounced the tramp and millionaire
With socialistic tests to roof the storm;
Panic moved the "redneck" for better air
That would to thunder of races conform.
When Jim Crow massed the blacks on back of train,
And sounds outside did all lynchings confirm,
Greenbacks on track became an "endless chain"
That strengthened Grover Cleveland's second term.

As hard times in the eighteen nineties piled,
Facing the panic, President stood mild.

Mohawks, 1890–1990

Mohawks refuse to put their weapons down
Or end casino gambling of their own;
For Indian affairs spoke Eddie Brown
To voice why from St. Regis all have flown.
Like eagles who to hawks might lose their nests
Their Warrior Society patrols;
They have with New York troopers met all tests
While tone of gunfire in distance rolls.
U.S. and Canada's officials meet
To silence sounds of rising revolution;
Mohawks on reservation might yet greet
Negotiation as their own solution.

Be it with problem Indian or Russian,
May warring now be fought by codiscussion.

Twentieth Century

Boundary Disputes

When Canada claimed Skagway as its own,
The U.S.A. demanded more at east;
When compromise by the "big stick" was shown,
Each in the other saw the tariff beast.
Since President with "Snow Lady" sought peace,
He for amendments all treaties withdrew;
Likewise in Caribbeans for increase
"Dollar Diplomacy" proved what he knew.
When Mexico against Diaz rebelled,
Who like a Czarist was an autocrat,
Henry Wilson by murder was expelled,
Leaving Woodrow the field that Taft left flat.

In nineteen twelve rose swell of urgency
For boundaries to quell insurgency.

Tri-Nation Republican Rulers

Great Britain, Canada, and U.S.A.
Formed dynasty republican to rule;
When Fenians forayed for separate way,
Canadian federation forked its fuel.
Dominion then extended sea to sea,
A northern neighbor grown to equal power;
Grant firmed Anglo-Americ-unity
By settling Alabama stress of hour.
Vote of tribunal international
Was victory for peace and arbitration;
It proved that by agreement rational
A global congress best may serve each nation.

As in new world three nations one would be,
So universe may rule with unity.

Nineteenth-Century Farming Recalled

The house of Grandma Moses seemed a barn
With a front porch and scroll work under eaves;
"Goin' to meetin'" ruled the prayer and yarn,
While horses for the family tree were leaves.
In North and West widened the country town
With church, high school, a barber shop, and bar;
But farming boy (with derby hat as crown)
On his buggy from girl was never far.
Famed spirit of farm life in print persists
With Freeman, Cather, Garland, and in verse;
Poor White of Sherwood Anderson exists
That all the mounts of fables will traverse.

The nineteenth-century farm and forestry
Were the strong building arm of industry.

Early Industry and Politics

The Middle West via ship tonnage spread
With millions of cargoes in 1901;
From Appalachian iron and coal bed
The global girth of factories was won.
Producers as rivals created pools
To divide enterprise and bank the price;
Combined as trusts with corporated tools,
They panged all politics for free franchise.
Commercial Interstate Act would declare
Some regulations to make fair the rates;
Americans imbued by laissez-faire
Gave individuals unfettered gates.

Complete freedom for each proved to be bleak
Before power of strong to wrong the weak.

Labor Organized

Trade unions of skilled workers multiplied
With immigrants and change to urban life;
Order of Knights of Labor then complied
To strike for due payment of all their strife.
As anarchists struck for eight-hour day,
A. F. of L. became the fighting spear;
Case of Sacco-Vanzetti proved the way
Labor injustice was to arts made clear.
As Justice Harlan wrote about *Adair,*
One may sell labor as person may feel;
Led by social concept of laissez-faire,
Organized labor struggled for square deal.

As Federation fought on all court banks,
It battled doctrinaires in its own ranks.

Recalling Nineteenth-Century Faith

Material creation builds a cross
For life on earth within eternity;
The Gilded Age for faith suffered no loss
Of either church or state paternity.
Rome would the "ghetto complex" give export
And not have priests with Protestants congressed;
But *Origin of Species* won support
For evolution that Darwin professed.
As controversy caused their faith to fall,
People did not for some time Bible read;
But Book that had to strong hearts given all
Stayed on the shelves for others who would lead.

The few who do the holocaust survive
Keep biblical portrait of Lord alive.

American Cultural Gateway

The Romanesque, Gothic, and Byzantine
Rose to the skyscraper in U.S.A.;
Science transmuted art to solid scene
With bridges joining every place and way.
Artists in life of people beauty sought,
As Eakins painted surgeons, fights, and games;
Drama and music then to vision brought
"The Stars and Stripes Forever" Sousa frames.
Fiction and poetry outlined for nation
What Whitman, Twain, Howells, and James portrayed;
Groups organized the young for education,
Who by science, Latin, and Greek were swayed.

The massive architecture of the past
At new American gateway was cast.

American Integration

As working day declined and leisure grew,
Americans found time for sports and games;
While some met for boat-racing to renew,
Others made track meets and ball fields their aims.
The joiners seeking fellowship approved
Fraternal orders and the D.A.R.;
Fox hunting, horse racing, and yachting moved
The yeoman farmer to share at the bar.
As sports extend the motion of the soul
To country clubs, horse shows, and smart hunt balls,
The parts of U.S.A. have become whole
As integration has worn off the walls.

As their equality courses conformity,
Americans grow free in uniformity.

Spanish-American War

To free Cuba U.S.A. warred with Spain,
Battling ten weeks on the Manila Bay;
Atlantic Squadron gunned the winning gain
That forced Spanish to terms of peace to sway.
Future of Philippines was all dispute
Until allegiance, 1964;
So-called Boxer Rebels could not refute
The U.S. policy of "open door."
Puerto Rico much like Cuba remains
A commonwealth of true self-government;
American conquest of Spain made gains
For islands with status made permanent.

With Teddy Roosevelt elected President
Post-Spanish War progress became more evident.

Theodore Roosevelt

As each the self to industry applied
With give-and-take for power organized,
Progressive Theodore Roosevelt supplied
The policy that his "Square Deal" advised.
A champion liberal conservative,
Hostile to malefactors of great wealth,
Teddy proved talent a preservative
For serving government with naught of stealth.
With trusts and trains maintained by regulation,
The tracks to Panama the leader cleared;
Expanding politics beyond the nation,
The President on stage of world appeared.

To spark the U.S. dreamed reality
Teddy torched, blazed, and beamed vitality.

William Taft

Victim of times and personality,
Betrayed by Progressives for tariff cause,
President Taft fought the monopoly
And gave Payne-Aldrich compromise applause.
As he reserved forests and the coal lands,
He strengthened states with the Mann-Elkins Act;
Reforming legislation at all hands,
Big Bill for progress was the silent fact.
Expanding law with two Amendments passed,
For legislation Taft made great reform;
But as some critics rate the first as last,
The uninformed would his genius deform.

As giants of the past swell history,
May William Taft dispel all mystery.

1912 Election

At Armageddon battling to be Lord,
Taft, Roosevelt, and Wilson led the fray;
While Teddy shrilled Old Testament accord,
Woodrow hyped up the heart with a New way.
The 1912 three-cornered contest moved
The limping elephant to an old Home;
Elected President, Wilson then proved
How Athens once had changed for rising Rome.
Woodrow Wilson would nation lift again
With the first standards set with love and pride;
Shifting the "Bull Moose thunder" from the rain,
He shined leaders with sun on every side.

Since vote of 1912 social justice assured,
America on globe as leader has endured.

Woodrow Wilson

High-minded, clean and strong, but cold of blood,
Woodrow Wilson steered social legislation;
As he the sea helped crews by union flood,
He sailed for banks and tariffs of the nation.
With Federal Reserve Act he towed each trust,
And with Clayton he chartered labor free;
For workers, farmers, and children a must,
Cooperation coursed his presidency.
As he moved patiently with Mexico,
He dealt with wealth and racial segregation;
Brooking conflicts with unity to flow,
Woodrow was a great leader of the nation.

Woodrow Wilson gave heights to all state rights
That brought new lights to centralize all sights.

First American View of World War I

War in Europe in nineteen fourteen shocked
America with horror and disgust;
Like a stone mountain by the thunder rocked
To keep some shape its strength became a must.
Neutral and pacifist, people were trees
That on hillside waved equally each branch;
But winds of Allies blew to storm the breeze
That shook each eastern house and western ranch.
Controversy over its neutral rights
Might have kept U.S.A. in its own yard;
But as more distant hills fell from their heights,
Americans their own fence had to guard.

When German patriots sang "Hymn of Hate,"
Kipling replied "The Hun is at the gate."

Neutrality

As Germany would the Allies defeat,
It by blockade kept power of the sea;
Americans from war preferred retreat,
Guarding their wealth with firm neutrality.
When a U-Boat the *Lusitania* sank,
Horror to U.S.A. gave a new sight;
Wilson with words gave warring his full rank,
Claiming that there were none "too proud to fight."
Problem of defense is to be prepared,
As Navy League did the Congress advise;
With Woodrow's reelection nation shared
The need to mediate and compromise.

Though for neutrality America stood strong,
For world equality it would not bear the wrong.

Wafts of War, 1917

When Wilson asked for peace and end of war,
Bethmann-Hollweg would have him caught by trap;
Peace Without Victory—Woodrow sought more
For silent mass in globe-united map.
As Germans threatened to sink submarines,
U.S. would not respond with "overt acts";
"To turn the other cheek" to warring scenes
The President would do while seeking facts.
Zimmerman Note revealed the underground
Of espionage for stirring Mexico;
So public cry for war became the sound
That echoed Russian rebels with full blow.

As Wilson versed freedom lost with neutrality—
"The world must be made safe" for all equality.

Approach to War by Sea

On April sixth of nineteen seventeen
U.S.A. declared war on Germany;
With Panama and Cuba bordering scene,
West would fight Austria in harmony.
With convoy system aiding U.S. troops,
Crossing Atlantic became safe and fast;
Congress created fleet to bridge the loops
With France to join each bursting U-Boat blast.
Some Yankee troops landed at Liverpool,
Others posting in France, mostly at Brest;
Only three escort vessels lost their cool,
While German hundreds were sunken to rest.

At sea the best method was the convoy
That could the prowling submarines destroy.

U.S. Expeditionary Force (1917–1918)

To train Americans for "over there"
Was like flocking of eagles to one band;
The sound of volunteers tuned all the air
As Expeditionaries left the land.
While A.E.F. knotted "over the top,"
Army and navy air-armed for the war;
With "pusher" biplanes flying as one crop,
Maneuvering controlled the near and far.
Offensive squadron before Argonne grew
With tripled size of flocks screeching in skies;
Thousands of U.S. airmen rose and flew
After the nine J-2's made the first rise.

Over first Expeditionary Force
Super-cheerleader Wilson aired the course.

American Opinion War

With propaganda driving near and far
Opinion was for President the field;
To hate the enemy and love the war
Was for the people hence their only shield.
With Espionage and the Sedition Acts
Congress made battlefield of neighborhood;
Destroying German print and air-sound facts
Led local feuds to be not understood.
A victory on home front was by food,
As U.S. "Hooverized" breadstaffs and meats;
To feed the Allies was the nations' mood
With unity that all wrangling defeats.

America with freedom, faith, and gold
With unity of self could others hold.

Pro Pacem League of Nations

Peace Conference with Armistice was viewed
By Allies whose demands became extreme;
Though Treaty of Versailles tyrants subdued,
Hot strength of Germany still steamed the stream.
Statesmen of Europe with Wilson agreed
That settlement be international;
Resulting League of Nations hence decreed
What made cooperation rational.
With membership open to all dominions
Seeking security and global peace,
The League absorbed self-governing opinions
That would for independence have release.

All colonies that were as booty held
For welfare of natives the League upheld.

Isolation versus Liberalism

Wilson would to his death for Treaty fight
As he through Middle and Far West professed;
When by thrombosis forced into the night,
He gave Palmer some days as he progressed.
Woodrow would "not let this country see red"—
Thus antiradical Quaker campaigned;
Sacco-Vanzetti case hence brought to head
The body with which liberals had reigned.
Hate literature of angry groups exposed
The isolation of who would be free;
Political parties became disposed
To welcome liberals within country.

To answer *What Price Glory* with a *Farewell to Arms*
The patriot of story exposes all alarms.

Twentieth-Century Dawn of Change

As nineteen hundred opened on the range,
The melting pot stood bubbling for release;
U.S.A. unified for a great change
In law and politics for war or peace.
As rising sun brightened the width of field,
People found roads for riding Model T;
Motors forced all competitors to yield
In race of sales of what each claimed to be.
With the petroleum of underground,
Land owners motored engines to "strike oil";
As advertisers phrased the rising sound,
America rode fast on its own soil.

What twentieth century for growth had stocked
Auto and ad men at the gate unlocked.

Rising by Air

For engines to apply to aviation
Science had to teach people how to fly;
Aerodynamics gripped the mind of nation
That sought to grapple bird flights in the sky.
At Kitty Hawk the Wright brothers outlined
The conquest of the air above each tower;
Promoters, writers, and students combined
For wing design, control, and applied power.
Pulled by the war from "sailcloth, stick and string,"
U.S. aircraft coped with heaven and earth;
With aviation rising wing on wing,
America gave global flight its birth.

Some day each family will have to be on guard
For helicopter on the roof, the porch, or yard.

Restricted Immigration

Southern and eastern Europe immigration
Caused labor leaders to fear their wage gains;
As flocks of eagles would cause dove deflation,
The settled birds planned to protect their plains.
Women like sparrows rose in revolution
To soar where they had never been before;
True "thoroughbreds" in their own constitution,
They faced challenge of new forest for more.
On quota basis immigration laws
Restricted aliens to reefed racial nests;
Branching on trees above all tempest flaws,
Household fliers with new wings met all tests.

Restricting immigration cannot confine the nation
Where marriages ration the eternal creation.

Spreading Sports

As poet gives to verse the beat and rhyme
And reader moves by thought or starts to sway,
Americans for sports give leisured time
Either to watch or with others to play.
Boxing, football, baseball, and race of horse,
Or watching games of others on T.V.—
All stir the public fast to join the course,
Each to play golf, tennis, or bowl, or ski.
The sports of gentlemen in U.S.A.
To a profession of nation have grown;
For those who work the games are now a way
To make the joy of living all their own.

Though not Dempsey, Babe Ruth, or Man O'War,
Each Jack and Jane may sport like any star.

Flaring Feminism

Morals of First World War defrosted lives
That to freezing of sex would not respond;
Protestant ethics iced widows and wives,
While "chippies" with disease melted the pond.
As prophets Freud, Ellis, and Jung had versed,
Psychology might have passion contained;
The girls with boys as equals hence conversed,
As they *This Side of Paradise* sustained.
America sparked sexual revolution
That left old principles darkened and bare;
Rising with rights equaled by Constitution,
Women stood up with their own torch to flare.

Females at the frontier flashed from the underworld
With flag of liberty on lake of life unfurled.

Wall Street Annexes

Combustion engine and airplane moved time
To measure Antarctic at the North Pole;
But crash of stock market depressed the clime
That "open door" had Wall Street held as goal.
Debunking became literary mode,
Poets proclaiming U.S.A. "waste land";
Mencken made "booboisee" the common code,
But novelists and playwrights rose to stand.
Broadcasting spread good music and jazz tones,
While scholarship and science came of age;
Medicine, physics, and the books were stones
That built the canopies of the new stage.

Annexed to depression that nation changed,
High mounts American for world still ranged.

Ohio Ganged Harding

The nineteen twenties canned a cunnng crop
In Congress crewed with rumbling hollow men;
Game-hunters orating in global hop,
They pounced like pirates in a preacher's den.
The times had one Harding, the best of lot,
Nice "spieler" who had all of favors done;
With his "Ohio gang," loyal and hot,
He moved as President to Washington.
That Warren G's was the most raffish "court"
Has been proclaimed by some of history;
How he a "good fellow" had such a sort
Remains to patriots a mystery.

From grasping gang Harding had none release,
A helping heart bursting with beats for peace.

Trials of Twenties

By conference and peace pacts U.S. moved
To serve the warring world by incantation;
With will to feed others the nation grooved
American Relief Association.
People for people urged Near East Relief,
While Congress for Europe war debts released;
But Nicaragua stirred volcanic grief
That with Sandino a Cesar produced.
With F.D.R. "good neighbor" way to strive,
Stimson with Philippine leaders embraced;
Friendly relation proved what stays alive,
The unity that future peace has paced.

As trials of twenties were by treaty won,
May global wars with talk sessions be done.

Calvin Coolidge

In years of loud shouting old-aging boys
One "silent Cal" with gracious lady ruled;
With the fine art that quiet mind employs
He by veto wild speculators cooled.
Like the oak trees that with leaves fed the grass
That he had forested near Vermont fields,
President Coolidge dropped upon the mass
The mulch of faith that a good harvest yields.
Winning people by personality,
Calvin was "President in his own right";
Rising "Republican prosperity"
Boomed for C. C. all economic might.

In age of pretension, extravagance, and noise
Coolidge soothed the tension by strength of quiet poise.

Herbert Hoover

America with Herbert Hoover boomed
As dreams of freed people appeared as real;
Brokers and investors in nation bloomed
For harvesting of millions as ideal.
H. H., humanitarian the most,
Had in wartime distributed the food;
For the commerce department from his post
He gave to business a mounting mood.
Born on Iowa farm, he earned his way
To engineering commerce like a grad;
When for global relief he gave each day
All saw in him the living Galahad.

Hoover to leadership brought social type
With expertise that handled help or hype.

The Great Depression

When on Black Thursday the stock market crashed
It started downward slide to bottom rock;
Mountain of wealth, on poor foundation hashed,
Fell to depression with a global shock.
The hills of commerce crumpled everywhere
While farms, resorts, and banks fell into dust;
The laissez-faire that breezed all of the air
Made public plans for rebuilding a must.
When Hoover tented back in thirty-three
He cleared the camp for twentieth-century crop;
The desperate kept faith in their country
Where no fascists nor communists could hop.

Depressed Americans wandered about
For leadership to show which way was out.

Franklin D. Roosevelt

Franklin D. Roosevelt hoisted each arm
That bore the torch above depression glade;
Ambition warmed with jauntiness and charm
Heated each speech the happy warrior made.
With a New Deal for the "forgotten man"
He won the strongest mandate of the nation;
With trumpet call for fear of fear to ban
He stirred for leadership a re-creation.
When he for people called by "action now"
Power to war the depressed situation,
Firmed F. D. R. was instrument of how
Congress was bent to mass determination.

As sparrows sometimes meld with crows to fly,
With F. D. Roosevelt the flocks rose high.

New Deal

Fireside chats warmed nation to New Deal
From White House that became a country home;
The "brain-trusters," a cabinet most real,
Helped F. D. R. lift all walls to a dome.
With Square Deal and New Freedom dealt to all,
Old cards became unstacked for common hands;
Giving to each the right to move or stall,
The President gave players no commands.
Rules set by farm and labor legislation
Rounded domestic program of the Deal;
Established nature of the game for nation
Made hope of winning for each one be real.

New Deal proved that for those who most would dare
What becomes highest wisdom is to share.

TVA

After first "Hundreds Days" of Roosevelt Acts
Through the Red Sea to sight of promised land,
The TVA conserved with best contracts
What would for poor confirm a working hand.
As program for the people became grand
Its concept like a mighty river flowed;
Its force electric over fertile land
A sparkling life of great enhancement showed.
Tennessee Valley with Authority
Gave from phosphates to all the needs for farm;
By giving dams and parks equality
It braced all private industry with arms.

As TVA made private income grow,
It gave to socialism not a show.

Anti-Rooseveltians

Fascists and communists in nation grew,
Extremists claiming F. D. R. had failed;
But radio priests like Coughlin were not few
Who as "Christ's deal" the presidency hailed.
Between two poles all sought depression cure
With varied "small, sour, and angry" themes;
Some demagogues like "King fish" Long were sure
They could the nation stir by subtle schemes.
Words "Share-the-wealth" became a mighty force,
Crowds yelling "Double-Crossing President";
Response of President firmed faith and course
That most as mercy of new Deal had felt.

All pitch and volume Franklin toned to fix
Firm responses for vote in thirty-six.

New Deal Opposition

With honeymoon over in thirty-four
Finance and business to grief arose;
Starry-eyed profs and bureaucrats no more
Could like Stalin and Hitler stand as foes.
Like Horatius tycoons faced fearful odds,
Liberty League expressing passing theme;
For each to touch "the temple of the gods"
One would not make the government supreme.
Social Security reached Supreme Court
That from its pose began to make retreat;
Once more, with Constitution as their fort,
Dissenters were majority at seat.

New Deal spawned both the demagogues and cranks
To stir the young and jobless to their ranks.

1936 Election

Campaign of thirty-six flamed to the sky
As Landon sparked Republicans with heat;
To save the U.S. way they claimed to try
By burning despotism at its seat.
Despite predictions of the polls and news
Roosevelt fired grass to great landslide;
To dust the ashes people rose in crews,
Except Maine and Vermont who stood aside.
The victor F. D. R. by acclamation
Renewed for nation its discovery;
Americans rule by their proclamation
That freedom forges all recovery.

New victory gave Franklin a strong fort
To light his mandate at the Supreme Court.

New Deal Conclusion

Fair Labor Standards Act the workers pleased
With happiness, efficiency, and health;
Nearby in Canada most were appeased,
Led by MacKensie King to share the wealth.
Against division of the native land
The reservation Indians stood firm;
As to redskins the New Deal stretched its hand,
Equality for blacks it would confirm.
The governmental functions in expanse
Revised the economic life of nation;
The interests of people to advance
Concluded all of New Deal's declaration.

Democracy that weathered Great Depression
Was greatest hope of problems in progression.

Approaching Storm of World War II

Fanatic Adolph Hitler heaved with hate
Of Christians, Jews, and all democracy;
He pressed Austrians and Czecks to annexed fate
With faked appeasement of autocracy.
Distant storming Japan on China cracked,
Breaking all commerce with the U.S.A.;
Meanwhile German "Blitzkrieg" the Poles attacked,
Leaving Britain alone in winds to sway.
Winston Churchill with "blood, toil, tears, and sweat"
Flashed lightning to new world to save the old;
Never to flag nor fail for freedom set,
He would face thunder with the brave and bold.

America would move with urgency
Equal to storm of the emergency.

Pearl Harbor

Events in Far East made all tensions mount
As Japanese warlords sought full control;
When the issues to crisis started count,
Negotiations sparred with loss of toll.
Though Hull sought Tojo to leave China clear,
The minister on ultimatum set;
Chiang Kai-shek aid had stirred Japan with fear
That U.S. would the East by power net.
Determined to destroy Pacific Fleet
With no warning of war they would declare,
From Kurile Islands armed for them to meet
Japs moved to conquest they would make by air.

December seventh nineteen forty-one
Air raid, Pearl Harbor as no drill was done.

Turning Tide of 1942

American Joint Chiefs of Staff took hold
With strategy of strong active defense;
Like banging of the "Shangri-La" of old,
Assault on Tokyo aired the offense.
Battle of Coral Sea, May, forty-two,
Made Japanese turn back from their mistakes;
Yamamoto with carriers tried to do
What Nagumo would also fail for stakes.
U.S. dive-bombers made carriers explode,
So that the Jap commanders could not stay;
The Stars and Stripes were given flying code
By victory of Battle of Midway.

The turn of tide was not the real finale
Before New Guinea and Guadalcanal.

Guadalcanal and On

Guadalcanal with Airsols in command
Made Japanese by U.S. meet defeat;
Meanwhile, with coast of Papua in hand,
Counteroffensive avoided retreat.
The lights of victory viewed "second front"
In Africa past Operation "Torch";
The Darlan Deal led Allies to confront
Problems of Casablanca on its porch.
To invade Sicily was the next move
To protect house from Rommel's Afrika Korps;
Montgomery and Bradley fought to prove
That victory of Cape Bon roofed for more.

North Africa, from enemy once cleared,
With its soft underbelly hence appeared.

Invasion of Italy

Supply subs the German U-Boats increased
To make the operation "Torch" burn long;
Sparks of the "Overlord" were thus decreased,
While plans to flicker Sicily shone strong.
With General Eisenhower in command
Fifth Army entered Naples to reach Rome;
With Anzio past, Eighth Army stormed the land
To win Monte Cassino, floor to dome.
While roads to Rome in June of forty-four
Led troops to rush who would in city be,
No news could have intensed the action more
Than that Allies were coasting Normandy.

Atlantic to Pacific changed the call
That made plans for invading Europe stall.

Pacific Leap-Frogging

Japan held islands from a central point—
Bismarcks-Gilberts, Marshalls, and Carolines;
MacArthur's navy leap-frogged every joint,
While Turner and Spruance crushed all the spines.
When Battle of Philippine Sea began,
Hellcat fighters diverted Japan's fleet;
Ozawa, turning to the sea to span,
Was by surprise forced with Spruance to meet.
With one-day war of antiaircraft fire
The Japanese dropped hundreds of their planes;
Lost Marianas forced them to retire,
While Nimitz leap-frogged over wider lanes.

That Japs were beaten was clear to the wise,
But for resistance they would still advise.

Europe Invaded

Bombing German cities wasted each way,
Costing hundreds of thousands Allied lives;
Ike Eisenhower's Normandy D-Day
Gave to air war the winds on which it thrives.
Battle went on to July twenty-four,
British at Caen, U.S.A.'s at Saint Lo;
With six-weeks' victory in France and more,
Allies to invade Germany would go.
Since Patton overran Rheims and Verdun,
The Germans lost last line in valley Po;
The warring on the western front was won,
But in the south logistics promised woe.

With clearing of the way to Antwerp doomed,
Another winter of campaign was loomed.

Leyte Gulf

October twenty-fifth in forty-four,
Where once Magellan with his ships had sailed,
At Leyte Gulf, greatest sea fight of war,
America with air support prevailed.
Surigao Strait Battle Japs first led
From Samar and Engano to retreat;
As Jesus on third day rose from the dead,
Battle at part three overcame defeat.
With Philippine waters thus in command,
U.S. Navy could any challenge face;
Like force that truth and justice may demand
They sailed the waters with a gloried grace.

Though enemy fought Gulf for two months more,
MacArthur's hands caught all who came ashore.

U.S.E.

United States of Europe soon will be
A union of people equal by law;
Each nation as a part of one country
Will from others be free more strength to draw.
The Europeans a vision embrace
Of unity with treaties doubly pledged;
They must for politics share greater space,
With their economy equally edged.
Having in Rome met in community,
Countries for solidarity resolve;
It may the greatest dream of century be
That Europe as one nation will evolve.

Be it for shared defense or single currency,
The oneness of Europe now moves with urgency.

Pre-Roosevelt Interlude

As Democrats sought peace as rational,
To "beat Germany first" some would reverse;
To fight Hitler all deemed irrational,
While of Pearl Harbor they chose to converse.
Republicans would "One World" organize,
Even at having to support the war;
But Roosevelt election helped advise
That people looked for peace both near and far.
Weary of Wallace who winged to the left,
The President with Harry Truman flew;
That isolationism was bereft
The voters and the politicians knew.

During third pre-Roosevelt interlude
Problems leading to war were a prelude.

Battling to Victory

Defense battles stormed nineteen forty-four
At Scheldt, Aachen, and the Ruhr river dams;
When Patton captured Metz, Lorraine, and more,
Campaign stretched forth along the Siegfried rams.
Bastogne with Battle of the Bulge was saved,
And Eisenhower to the Rhine advanced;
On Ruhr with greatest operation braved
The chance of Allied victory enhanced.
Through Poland, Germany, and Austria marched
The Allies, pulsed by Ike's eternal breath;
The lands that no fire of Hitler parched
Fell as the coward hustled his own death.

When Allied victory at Rheims was signed,
To end of war in West U.S. aligned.

Harry Truman

Born on the farm but to reap wheat and corn,
Truman by reading unmasked mystery;
In Presidency he by nature born
Harry shined the new fields of history.
Though postwar problems threatened with a shade,
He opened windows with a real "Fair Deal";
Campaign for civil rights of blacks he made,
As he large crowds addressed with great appeal.
"Pour it on, Harry!" was the spreading cry,
Beyond losses of all his party mates;
Like rising sun with new rays for the sky,
H. T. melted the keys of all the gates.

Chosen as President in his own right,
H. T. became the star of a dark night.

Iron Curtain

As Truman pronounced "I like Uncle Joe,"
The policy "be nice to Russia" ruled;
The audience with communists would grow
Until by restored "hard line" they were fooled.
The Potsdam and Yalta agreements failed,
As liberals gave Stalin full support;
With "Better Red than Dead" their voices hailed
As they to Iron Curtain gave rapport.
The minds of wisdom returned to research,
As each, a spatial sun, became a star;
Roost thermonuclear gave them the perch
From which to vision any future war.

As hot battle of tongues curtained its span,
The cold one on the opened stage began.

United Nations

U.S., Britain, Russia, and China met
In Washington in nineteen forty-four;
United Nations in New York then set
To fight aggression without force of war.
The International at Bretton Woods
Banked Reconstruction and Development;
Then for each nation to protect its goods
The Marshall Plan outlined a free ascent.
Eastern and Western countries union made,
America funding Europe's know-how;
Defeating all the tricks of Marxian trade,
Democracy made past move to the now.

Trades of United Nations balance more
The strokes and counterstrokes of a cold war.

Cold War

Storms broke in forty-seven, forty-eight,
Bursting fields of Iran, Turkey, and Greece;
Truman Doctrine moved to initiate
The rays that from coercion brought release.
In Palestine clouds clapped Arabs and Jews
With thunder of a never ceasing war;
In Europe strokes and counterstrokes were clues
Of communistic flashings near and far.
American and British airlift flew
High into heavens where the skies are clear;
With Captain Truman all the flights gave view
Of peace the force of NATO made appear.

Containment was the conquest of the bold
Who froze when winds of war all became cold.

Nixon Presidency

Richard Nixon no person would defend
Who in justice set self above the law;
With Crime Control and Safe Streets Act to bend
He gave *agents provocatures* the claw.
When CIA broke into Watergate
With phone taps to absorb all mystery,
The "caper" capped all news to activate
The worst disgrace in U.S. history.
Airing of secret documents and tapes
The Presidential cover-up exposed;
Obstruction of justice by worst of shapes
Impeachment case of Nixon thus imposed.

Since further scandal he could not afford,
Tricked Dick resigned his post to Gerald Ford.

Gerald Ford

For pardon and prestige to be restored
Like that of eagle returned to the nest,
Over to Presidency Gerald Ford
Flew to heal Watergate by all his best.
By "Law and Order" he proved country fair,
But rising prices closed the fields of oil;
With winds of Vietnam War still in the air,
G. F. was forced to walk on ravaged soil.
For strength of war and peacetime industry
The triumph over the Cambodians proved
More than caretaker President was he
Who peace by "shuttle diplomacy" moved.

That best of nations is the U.S.A.
Ford Program made secure in every way.

New Times, New Laws

States pass new laws their own problems to curb—
Drugs, cigarettes, and politician gifts;
Though rules for landfills may yet some disturb,
Recycling does to others give new lifts.
While sounds of war in other nations rise
And leaders wrestle over dates for peace,
In New Hampshire lawmakers authorize
Sentencing all "hate crimes" without release.
Whatever the sex, race, or faith may be,
No preferences will dominate the law;
Equality is dawn of liberty
Where once only the darkness people saw.

As East and West seek global brotherhood,
Nations embrace with laws of neighborhood.

U.S. Leadership

The Soviet Union takes U.S. advice
In dealing with crisis in Middle East;
Decade of radicals on global ice
Has forged no fusion of famine and feast.
Shevardnadze-Shamir in Washington
Gave Israel and Moscow stronger ties;
Regional arms control by discussion
Evolved with how the peace of future lies.
The forum with increased communication
Made Gulf Crisis the current holy cross;
Russian-American cooperation
Gives unity the rule without a loss.

As Israel and Arabs with the Soviets link
America leads all from any warring brink.

1990s Battlefield

America battled with threat of war
While sixteen other conflicts gunned the world;
For politics of country, faith, or more
Nations have held the flag of peace unfurled.
South Africa, Columbia, Kuwait,
Liberia, and Tibet resume arms;
In Guatemala, spurred with gruesome gait,
The army shoots and civic people harms.
Civilians more than soldiers have been killed
As farms and cities become battle grounds;
But more has famine than the gunfire stilled
As people tried to move from shooting sounds.

Let braves of 1990s be informed
That those who fall may not be uniformed.

Reviewing 1952 Election

Marked by malaise, suspicion, and frustration
With love of China and Korean course,
Truman seemed to strengthen the rogues of nation,
McCarthy and the Hess subversive force.
Years "scandalous," as printed *Look* reviewed,
Put Democratic malefactors in power;
But minds of intellect their hope renewed
With Adlai Stevenson as man of hour.
Above the public roofs there rose a tower
That put low factories of hate on strike;
Posting the flag for General Eisenhower,
The nation started singing "I Like Ike."

America in nineteen fifty-two
Voted for what a patriot would do.

President Dwight D. Eisenhower

Dynamic was conservatism phrased
As Eisenhower made people secure;
Equality in civil rights he raised
Like integrated scholarship made sure.
Humanitarian and man of peace,
The Refugee Relief Act he obtained;
With immigration quotas' great increase
He sought that communism be restrained.
"Atoms for Peace" proposed in Fifty-three
Would have U.S. with Soviet Russia bind;
To make uranium stockpiles equal be
Atomic power must be peaceful kind.

For "the miraculous inventiveness of man"
Nation endorsed what Dwight for world peace first began.

1950s Foreign Issues

Africa, Asia, Europe, Middle East
Were stages past direction of the play;
Actors for independence forged their feast
As Marxian communism fed the fray.
Two Matsu-Quemoy crises opened fire
While the Suez Canal the Nassers blocked;
In Lebanon U.S. managed the mire,
And plans for "summit meeting" hence were clocked.
As photographic flights in Russia flew
To spot cloaked nuclear activities,
Russians wondered how much U.S.A. knew
Of how they were prepared beyond treaties.

For war of bombs the Soviets were strong,
While they proclaimed Americans as wrong.

Carter Citation

Postpresidential period is most
The time when leadership really extends;
Thus Jimmy Carter became global host,
For who issues of liberty attends.
Man of many and diverse roles in act,
He toned most international disputes;
Populist for humanity by fact,
He rationed peace that world-warring refutes.
As *We the People 2000* excites
Freedom and equal rights on every shore,
Liberty Medal of Penn's City cites
What J. E. C. conserved by doing more.

By way America built its foundation
Jimmy Carter was hilt of roof of nation.

Ronald Reagan

As liberals become conservative
To maintain rights of people and of states,
So Ronald Reagan was preservative
For laws that give to freedom open gates.
For communist witch-hunts he dramatized
What feet beneath the witness table urged;
Democracy he never compromised
While favored moneyed interests upsurged.
Perhaps a President must actor be,
Meeting others with warm and smiling face;
One Ronald Reagan on both sides was free
While Democratic Action proved his grace.

As Ron on open stage played all extremes,
No climax compromised his theme of dreams.

Color-Blind Casting

Regardless of color, actor now speaks
The speech on stage by tripping tongue pronounced;
Multicultural, racial, and gender cheeks
Smile equally when casting is announced.
An Afro Scrooge in Arden Theatre stars,
And wife of Pericles is of dark hue;
As changing cultural landscape moves the bars,
Black Franchelle Dorn makes Lady Macbeth true.
Theater must be of universal space,
Stripping private identities to core;
Race, birth, and sexual face it must erase,
While it for mind and heart moves more to score.

Father may be Hispanic, mother black;
All equally now stage palace or shack.

George Bush

Let all have faith in President who knows
All strategy with latitude and length;
Like the great force above the wind that blows
George Bush has knowledge of all tested strength.
When Ronald Reagan stumped the role on stage
He led the act of national applause;
But the director who turned every page
Was he who knew for every move the cause.
A quiet scholar of all history,
Bush feels the storm Saddam Hussein would frame;
The claps of thunder are no mystery
Of how the tyrant would world theater flame.

G. B. with word sounds would hold back by breath
The bomb that bursts to unity by death.

Process Bush

Not lightly did U.S. to conflict drive,
As Bush the preconditions all had tried;
His brilliance led the President to strive
To keep nations by coalition tied.
George built and kept at home a full support
With which bipartisan Congress agreed;
With army men and women in rapport,
He moved to stop Saddam Hussein with speed.
When terms of peace S. H. with shrug despised,
G. B. coursed each complex with expertise;
Coalition of nations thus devised
What would bring the aggressor to his knees.

As Bush and supporters control the fray,
They all deserve our thanks and prayers each day.

Desert Storm

Allied U.S. attacked Iraq, Kuwait,
With aircraft having launched wave after wave;
The Desert Storm moved with a global gait
As countries thunder for their skies to save.
Twenty-eight nations in effort unite
Against mad Iraqi Saddam Hussein;
For restored calm in Persian Gulf as sight
They view George Bush as their first flash to gain.
America, superior and brave,
Again moves with courage of leadership;
The desert is for tyranny the grave
Beneath airmen with war clouds in their grip.

Storm in the Gulf once more makes evident
The advanced admiralship of President.

Warriors in the Gulf

Allies of Europe praised the U.S.A.,
Applauding raids and vowing their support;
Turkish air bases opened on the way;
Japan promised its forces to export.
While Italy its powers authorized,
Some Germany wavered with hesitation;
Though Spanish ships were but logistics sized,
Thatcher for Washington offered her nation.
As Gorbachev blamed stiff Saddam for war,
And Dumas called Hussein a self-walled mate,
Gulf nations willed America to star
As defender of people of each state.

When Iraqi refused to pull out of Kuwait,
Warriors in the Gulf as U.S. aid stood straight.

History and the Persian Gulf

The use of history voices debate
On current war Congress had to decide;
With Socrates and Lincoln pared to rate,
Madison, Churchill, and the Saints abide.
Like Mussolini and Hitler appeased,
And Tonkin Gulf entangling Vietnam war,
The subjects of the past in some way eased
The need to know what we are fighting for.
History computes the fractioned world for change
With "vision and forbearance" viewed by Lee;
Parceled at Persian Gulf all must arrange
To fight Saddam Hussein with unity.

Ideas become events in move to a solution
As bombing is intense in cause of Constitution.

Crackling Desert Storm

The clouds that crackle thunder moved from past
When moisture from the ground rose to the sky;
Hussein by banging Kuwait self would cast
That he like Egypt's Nasser be judged by.
Iraq battled Iran for eight, hard years,
Supported by profits of Kuwait oil;
But when Saddam could grease no more his gears,
He moved closer for chunks of nearest soil.
S. H. is not the magnet Nasser flamed
Nor lightning that U.S. with rod prevents;
As storming war of air he has defamed,
He to the ground encounters thus consents.

As the attacks on Israelites increased,
So Desert Storm its stronger strikes released.

Operation Desert Storm

Most complex battling action since D-Day,
Now Desert Storm wars beyond history;
The seven nations, joined with U.S.A.,
Strike sites of Iraqi with accuracy.
As Air Force F-15's with Navy flew
To escort Saudi aircraft on runway,
The combined action proved what Horner knew
That single "air-taking" orders the way.
As Operation Storm veers victory,
It thunders from a clear chain of command;
It rings it right for the military
With pin-point timing of the ruling hand.

For conquest in the air with plan precise
Storming of desert needs but one advice.

Miscalculator Hussein

To be first Arab to face super power,
Martyred with Iraq (his own inspiration),
Hussein corrupted language of the hour
With "enemies of God" as Western nation.
Dividing Iran, Lebanon, Kuwait,
And scudding Israel to wider war,
The cruel zealot gave to fear full weight
That future would flash flames of battle more.
Attacks of SCUD missiles unjustified
As victory were a miscalculation;
When to the peace term he never replied,
Saddam misjudgment led to complication.

What Hussein gave to warring with his brush
He would learn from the conflict with George Bush.

Moral and Just Gulf War

Addressing clergymen, Bush spoke with strength,
A current angel singing for the Lord;
He gave the words "moral" and "just" full length
For height to which the Gulf defense has soared.
Is it "moral" to help Kuwait by force?
The President replied for firm defense;
A "just" war must a noble cause enforce—
To battle for world peace is no offense.
Let all recall that plunder of Kuwait
Was like that of Hitler on Polish ground;
Though Bush does not seek war, he will not wait
For gunning by Hussein to drown all sound.

Gulf war shows how the right must stand before the wrong;
In face of tyranny human freedom is strong.

Communicated Truth on Desert Storm

Despite the stench and mire of the news,
The President with force of facts appears;
His knowledge gives the course to global crews
Who for the people battle without fears.
As once a George faced Old World with his sword,
His namesake operates the Desert Storm;
America at war fights for the Lord
To prove the den of peace is not a dorm.
G. B. for all the globe has stayed awake,
Knowing the why and when each nation moves;
His strength of expertise controls each take
As truth of his communication proves.

As fire flames bandits with oil from Mars,
The Almighty shines Bush to glow with stars.

Antiwar Activists

Dictators like Hussein no questions leave
That people must by might battle for peace;
Antiwar strategy becomes naive
When it for problems offers no release.
We ask what is alternative to war
While all as one would smash evil Saddam?
To "bring the troops home now" would but restore
The tram by giving it the ground to ram.
Antiwar activists conservative
Find that they cannot always peace proclaim;
Gulf strategy has no alternative
That would their lack of responses explain.

As Generals battle for the air and ground once more,
Antiwar movements fight against the final war.

One-Day Occupation

A one-day war could map battles to come
For Islamics against the Jewish state;
When Iraqi marched to Khafji with drum,
U.S. Marines and the Saudis met fate.
A tool political for print and view,
The fighting hammered sounds of rising storm;
With thunders that from Arab desert blew
Hussein at the war front displayed his form.
Saddam moved to arouse the Arab world
With both Algeria and Jordan bound;
When he to call Iran his flag unfurled,
The Jewish state began to hear his sound.

The one-day play might yet have been the way
To ease assaults of conflict in the fray.

Infernos of War

Ventura, the North Sea, and Mexico
Have blazed the hottest fires of oil wells;
Those of Kuwait have been the inferno,
A problem that for world may toll all bells.
The scorched earth policy of mad Hussein,
Inflamed by the allied bombing attacks,
Has surfaced what is the internal pain
That peace of people constantly retracts.
Humanity must rid itself of hate
In competition of who flies above;
Equality achieves the highest rate
When measured one to one in globe of love.

May we and Iraqui seek God the more
For unity forever free form war.

Winning War or Peace

When war is done, who is winner of peace?
The bombs still blow in battle of ideas;
The flow of wealth must have global release,
While social justice guides more than careers.
Hussein once tried three Big Ideas to sell—
The Palestinians, regions, poor-rich fray;
But Israel and U.S. tolled the bell
Of war so peace in Persian Gulf would stay.
No "intifada" Arab hostility
Turned victory to a disarmed defeat;
Because regions are held politically,
The battles of ideas from war retreat.

The eagle that will all for doves release,
America wins wars for lasting peace.

Contemplating Vietnam War

Soldiers committed to U.S. defense
Are not always given a full support;
Congress may put a conquest on the fence
While President is tied to weak export.
Lesson of Vietnam has to history taught
That warriors move with public consent;
When use of military force is sought,
Senate must willingly give full assent.
Frustration that over Vietnam arose
Led to enact War Powers Resolution;
An action that the hands of leader froze
Clouded the courses of the Constitution.

Nation for dynamism to restore
Proved to be lesson of the Vietnam War.

Persian Gulf War Patriots

When Patriots the Scud offense defeat
They strengthen dream of a missile-proof shield;
As tyrants like Hussein would whole world beat,
Defense is more important than to yield.
When Reagan unveiled use of SDI,
He foresaw method of Iraqi threat;
As tyrant would the ICBM's try,
The need to defend people hence was set.
Defensive weapons can terror restrain
Like Patriots that Scud missiles control;
Brutal oppressor like Saddam Hussein
Must not his strength by force make globe extol.

Hail Patriots in the Persian Gulf War,
American heroes forever more!

Living Agony

My heart is dripping blood from growing pain,
As I upon our culture contemplate;
Where once America primed every plain
Its flops of feces now all desecrate.
Though once its women clothed with dignity
And men were recognized by bow and tie,
The people now undress for all to see
How much for sex each is ready to lie.
Where is the nation that fought for ideals
For which each might be equally the king?
Is flesh alone the only thing that feels
What once ruled heart and mind in everything?

Dear God, give me the patience here to live
With strength of truth that only You can give.

American Decline?

A bullet dispelled myth of Camelot;
Then Martin Luther King, Jr. lay dead;
The nation tripped in Southeast Asia rot,
Sinking U.S. for three decades of dread.
Demoralized by loss of arms and oil
While the Pacific rimmed markets of nation,
America "seemed" to decline in foil
While being forced to endure some "stagflation."
Crime and corruption coursed with weakened schools
While country lost in nuclear power and space;
But all these conflicts were the parried pools
Of the great lake where faith would win the race.

United States can all problems survive
While it keeps will for victory alive.

Pro America

God bless America and keep it strong,
Land of the good, the beautiful, the true!
When it gives heart and head to right the wrong,
May it be loved for all that it can do.
Allies prepare to bomb Iraqi troops
While U.S. airplanes conquer all the skies;
Saddam Hussein then heaves from hidden loops
With terrorism that with slander flies.
As U.S.A. gives Europe aid once more,
That they in future may be strong and free,
We prove that in going beyond one's door
Who helps a friend thus earns an enemy.

It matters not how much is its own loss,
America for others bears the cross.

J. C.

In equalizing strength of hand and mind
Initial signs may seem the same to be;
Caesar and Christ are each a special kind,
Though both may be initialed as J. C.
Late into night voices speak from T.V.,
Led by choices of *Johnny Carson* show;
The quality of people shapes to be
Whatever leaders want others to know.
The world of Julius still runs battle fields,
While that of Jesus at His altar kneels;
But where both heart and mind the person yields
One there without true faith stumbles and keels.

May all for reaching heaven try to be
Worthy of preaching leaven of J. C.

Daily Prayer

Dear Lord, I pray Thee keep me firm in form
To recognize Thy force in all I say;
Whatever be the current human storm,
Please shine Your truth for us with daily ray.
In these the times when all order is bent,
Be it for force or writing poetry,
All those defying Thy divine consent
Would like Saddam Hussein a power be.
Dear God, please by my constant metaphor
That I would phrase by words in beat and rhyme;
Let roll of days prove to the world once more
That art like heaven rules the shapes of time.

No broken statement nor unfinished phrase
Echoes The Voice in daily prayer of praise.

Sempre America

The worlds may turn and nations come and go
While people seek the real of every dream;
America rises above all flow,
A pool eternalized with global stream.
In U.S.A. humanity has found
The what and when there swells up with the how;
It matters not the color, size, nor sound,
Each person brooks all history with now.
As heaven touches every bank and beach,
One sanctioned land shores all beyond all fears;
With good, the beautiful, and true in reach,
This nation has moved on five hundred years.

Sempre America will do for every crew
What Christopher captained in fourteen ninety-two.

Sail On and On!

Keep sailing, Christopher, for U.S.A.
With truth that heaven here on earth is real;
All like Americans would be today
To navigate the dream of the ideal.
As you touched ground to prove the world is round,
All people now your trip would imitate;
This unknown dome of deity you found
Is what all want though some envy with hate.
As eagles from their nests needed to fly,
You, brave leader, from old yard had to sail;
Since you circled the globe to view the sky,
For unity, Columbus, we all hail!

C. C., having proved what all moves upon,
We now with you will all sail on and on.

Columbian Hymn

As all people now to Columbus sing,
Each voice in its own way thanks the good Lord;
From sea to sea the bells of glory ring
With sounds that for all nations have a chord.
When Christopher sailed left to find the right
To prove in universe the globe is round,
The land that in the ocean rose to sight
Became the home for who its freedom found.
Each one with Christopher Columbus lives
Who does the most that hand and mind can do;
The search for heaven to U.S.A. gives
The faith first proved in fourteen ninety-two.

Whole world Columbian in nineteen ninety-two
Hails one America good, beautiful, and true.